PRINCE

The world premiere of a new British musical

Book and Lyrics by Phil Willmott
Music by Phil Willmott and Mark Collins

FINBOROUGH | THEATRE

First performed at the Finborough Theatre: Wednesday, 30 March 2016

Princess Caraboo was commissioned and developed in collaboration with Bristol Old Vic under the Artistic Directorship of Tom Morris with dramaturgy by James Peries and originally presented in a staged reading as part of Vibrant – A Festival of Finborough Playwrights.

PRINCESS CARABOO

Book and Lyrics by Phil Willmott
Music by Phil Willmott and Mark Collins

Cast

Princess Caraboo	**Nikita Johal**
Eddie Harvey	**Christian James**
Sir Charles Worrall	**Phil Sealey**
Lady Elizabeth Worrall	**Sarah Lawn**
Lord Marlborough	**Oliver Stanley**
Osvaldo Agathias	**Joseph O'Malley**
Mrs Catesby	**Rebecca Ridout**
Hatty	**Hilary Murnane**
Richard	**Ruben Kuppens**
Betty	**Althea Burey**

England, 1820.

The performance lasts approximately two hours and thirty minutes.
There will be one interval of fifteen minutes.

Director	**Phil Willmott**
Musical Director	**Freddie Tapner**
Choreographer	**Thomas Michael Voss**
Lighting Designer	**Jack Weir**
Set Designer	**Toby Burbidge**
Costume Designer	**Penn O'Gara**
Stage Manager	**Mary Alex Staude**
Assistant Director	**Adam Haigh**
Producers	**Joel Fisher**
	Li Vinall
Sound Designer	**James Nicholson**
Production Photographer	**Scott Rylander**
Orchestration and Arrangements	**Mark Collins**

Althea Burey | Betty
Trained at Colchester Institute and Guildford
School of Acting.
Theatre includes *Pandora* (Union Theatre) and
Don't Run (Waterloo East Theatre).
Theatre whilst training includes *Godspell,
Oklahoma!* and *Hands On A Hardbody*.

Christian James | Eddie Harvey
Trained at Central School of Speech and Drama.
Theatre includes *The Adventures of Pinocchio*
(Greenwich Theatre) and *Aladdin* and *Dick
Whittington* (Corn Exchange, Newbury).
Theatre whilst training includes *Twelfth Night,
Hamlet, Present Laughter, Company* and *Grease*.

Nikita Johal | Princess Caraboo
Trained at Performance Preparation Academy,
Guildford.
Theatre includes *Aladdin* (The Harlington, Fleet),
Bring It On: The Musical (Electric Theatre,
Guildford) and *The World Goes 'Round* (Yvonne
Arnaud Theatre, Guildford).
Voiceover includes *Kidzania* (London and Mexico).
Workshops include *Bend It Like Beckham*
(Dominion Theatre Studio) and *His Indian
Boyfriend* (Theatre Royal Stratford East).

Ruben Kuppens | Richard
Trained at Frank Sanders' Academy for Musical
Theatre and Guildford School of Acting.
Theatre includes *De Nieuwe IJstijd* (Dutch National
Tour), *Pandora* (Union Theatre), *Don't Run* and *IF*
(Waterloo East Theatre).
Theatre whilst training includes *Oklahoma!* and
Snoopy.

Sarah Lawn | Lady Elizabeth Worrall
Trained at Guildford School of Acting and Middlesex University.
Theatre includes *Blithe Spirit* (Gielgud Theatre), *Woman In Mind* (Vaudeville Theatre), *Peter Pan the Musical* and *Absent Friends* (Gordon Craig Theatre, Stevenage), *Season's Greetings* (Rhodes Art Complex, Bishops Stortford), *Anyone Can Whistle* (Bridewell Theatre), *Bless the Bride* (King's Head Theatre), *Sleeping Beauty* (Oxford Playhouse), *Around the World in Eighty Days* (Battersea Arts Centre), *Cinderella* (Cambridge Arts Theatre) and *Much Ado About Nothing, The Way of the World, A Funny Thing Happened on the Way to the Forum, Alice in Wonderland* and *The Country Wife* (UK Tours).
Film includes *Mumbo Jumbo*.

Hilary Murnane | Hatty
Trained at Mountview Academy of Theatre Arts.
Theatre includes *Hero and Amanda* (Canal Café Theatre) and *Orchid* (Etcetera Theatre).
Theatre whilst training includes *Mary Shelley, Bonnie and Clyde, Curtains, Parade, Chick, Fiddler on the Roof, The Bright and Bold Design, Romeo and Juliet* and *Titus Andronicus*.

Joseph O'Malley | Osvaldo Agathias
Trained at Guildford School of Acting.
Theatre includes *Women of Troy* (The Scoop), *One Man Two Guvnors* (National Theatre), *A Life of Galileo* (Royal Shakespeare Company), *Horrible Histories Tudors and Victorians, Horrible Histories Groovy Greeks, Horrible Science* (UK Tours), Billy (Union Theatre) and *HMS Pinafore* (King's Head Theatre).
Film includes *Natasha*.

Rebecca Ridout | Mrs Catesby
Trained at London School of Musical Theatre and National Youth Music Theatre.
Theatre includes *The Game* (St. James Studio Theatre), *A Christmas Carol* (Castle Theatre, Wellingborough), *Flight* (Opera Holland Park), *The Sound of Music* (Curve Leicester and International Tour), *Frances Ruffelle's Paris Original* (St. James Studio Theatre), *Love Is Eternal* (London Theatre Workshop), *The Next Big Thing* (Edinburgh Festival),

Molly Wobbly (Phoenix Artists Club) and *Tis the Season* (Jermyn Street Theatre).

Phil Sealey | Sir Charles Worrall
Productions at the Finborough Theatre include *Red Night*. Trained at Bristol Old Vic Theatre School. Theatre includes *Sondheim's Roadshow* (Union Theatre), *Dick Whittington* and *Aladdin* (Corn Exchange, Newbury), *Alice's Adventures Underground* (The Vaults), *Fanny and Stella* (Above the Stag Theatre), *The Ring Cycle Plays* (The Scoop), *The Searcher* (Greenwich Theatre), *The Winter's Tale* (Courtyard Theatre) and *Lord of the Flies* (Royal Shakespeare Company).

Oliver Stanley | Lord Marlborough
Trained at Birmingham School of Acting and Royal Academy of Music.
Theatre includes *Spring Awakening* (Loughborough Town Hall), *Billy Young* (Old Joint Stock Theatre, Birmingham), *Whistle Down The Wind* (Union Theatre), *Till The Clouds Roll By* (St. James Theatre), *Hair* (MacDonald Holyrood Hotel, Edinburgh) and *Evita* (UK Tour). Vocal performances at venues including the Prince Edward Theatre, St James Studio Theatre, Tower of London, Crazy Coqs, Café de Paris, The Actors' Church and the Hammersmith Apollo alongside Chris Martin and Coldplay.

Phil Willmott | Book, Lyrics and Music
Phil is one of the most sought-after musical theatre writers in the UK, developing commissions at Shakespeare's Globe, Bristol Old Vic, Liverpool Everyman and Playhouse, the National Theatre Studio, Theatre Royal Stratford East and for producers Adam Kenwright and Adam Spiegal. His past musicals include *Lost Boy* (Finborough Theatre and Charing Cross Theatre), *Secret Love* (National Tour), *Once Upon a Time at The Adelphi* (Liverpool, London and U.S.) and the widely and regularly revived *Dick Barton Trilogy, Around The World In Eighty Days* and *Jason And The Argonauts*. He is a multi-award winning director, artistic director, playwright, composer, librettist, teacher, dramaturg, arts journalist and occasional actor. He is founding Artistic Director of award winning theatre company The Steam Industry incorporating the Finborough Theatre (under the Artistic Directorship of Neil McPherson) and its sister organisation Gods and Monsters, producing London's annual Free Theatre Festival at the open-air amphitheatre The Scoop, on the South Bank. His international directing career incorporates

everything from classical drama, musicals and family shows to cabaret and cutting edge new writing. He is a recipient of a UK Theatre Award for outstanding direction of a musical, a Peter Brook Award for his outdoor classical productions and family shows, WhatsOnStage award nominations for best regional and Off West End productions, a Broadway World nomination for Best Musical in the UK, a Brooks Atkinson/Royal Court award in New York for Playwriting and four Spirit of Broadway awards.

Mark Collins | Music
Productions at the Finborough Theatre include Co-Composer for *Lost Boy* (which subsequently transferred to Charing Cross Theatre). Mark has also worked on many new musicals including: *The Secret Diary Of Adrian Mole* (The Curve, Leicester), *Dessa Rose* (Trafalgar Studios), Dougal Irvine's *The Other School* (St James' Theatre for National Youth Music Theatre), *Wah! Wah! Girls* (Kneehigh and Sadler's Wells at The Curve, Leicester; Peacock Theatre, London; and UK Tour) and Rifco's *Britain's Got Bhangra* (Theatre Royal Stratford East and UK Tour).
Mark is Assistant Musical Director for the West End production of *Billy Elliot The Musical* (Victoria Palace Theatre).

Freddie Tapner | Musical Director
Theatre includes *Jewish Legends* (Upstairs at the Gatehouse), *The Adventures of Pinocchio* (Greenwich Theatre), *H.R.Haitch* (Iris Theatre at St Paul's Church, Covent Garden), *Girlfriends* (Union Theatre) and *Dracula! (Mr Swallow – The Musical)* (Soho Theatre) which received a Chortle Music Comedy Nomination.
He is Principal Conductor for the London Musical Theatre Orchestra, and is currently Deputy on Keys-3 for *Wicked* (Apollo Victoria Theatre).

Thomas Michael Voss | Choreographer
Productions at the Finborough Theatre include *Princess Ida* for which he received an OffWestEnd nomination for Best Choreography. Theatre includes *Road Show* (Union Theatre), *Saturday Night* (Watermans Arts Centre), *A Little Night Music* (Trevor Nunn at Menier Chocolate Factory), *Twelfth Night* (The Space), *Spelling Bee* (Watermans Arts Centre) and *Finian's Rainbow* (Union Theatre and Charing Cross Theatre). He has also choreographed several TV commercials and internet viral videos for BBC's Strictly Come Dancing, Samsung, Westfield, Argos, Nintendo, P&O and Aunt Bessie's and music videos for Lily Allen, Craig David, Mark Ronson and James Blunt. He also teaches for Greenwich Dance, Dance Attic Studios, Crisis Charity and the Royal Academy of Dance.

Jack Weir | Lighting Designer

Productions at the Finborough Theatre include *Princess Ida, Three Guys Naked From The Waist Down* and *Armstrong's War*.

Trained at The Guildhall School of Music and Drama and recipient of the 2014 ETC Award for Lighting Design.

Theatre includes *Four Play* (Theatre503), *Bad Girls, Road Show, Fear and Misery* and *The Spitfire Grill* (Union Theatre), *African Gothic, Muswell Hill* (Park Theatre), *No Villain* (Old Red Lion Theatre), *My Children! My Africa!* (Trafalgar Studios), *Bruises* (Tabard Theatre), *The Sum of Us, Rise Like a Phoenix, Bathhouse, The Boys Upstairs* (Above The Stag Theatre), *All-Male Pirates of Penzance* (Hackney Empire and UK Tour), *Grim – The Musical* (Charing Cross Theatre), *Hamlet* (Riverside Studios), *Richard III* (Upstairs at The Gatehouse), *Passing By* (Tristan Bates Theatre) and *Titus Andronicus* (Arcola Theatre). www.weirdlighting.co.uk

James Nicholson | Sound Designer

Productions at the Finborough Theatre include *Lost Boy* which subsequently transferred to Charing Cross Theatre.

Trained at Central School of Speech and Drama.

Sound Designs include *Road Show, Lear, Ace of Clubs, Henry VI: Play of Thrones, White Feather* and *Fear and Misery of the Third Reich* (Union Theatre), *Ushers: The Front of House Musical* (Arts Theatre and Charing Cross Theatre), *As Is* and *Dessa Rose* (Trafalgar Studios), *Jacques Brel is Alive and Well and Living in Paris* and *Finian's Rainbow* (Charing Cross Theatre), *Shutters* (Park Theatre), *Made Up Stories from My Unmade Bed* (BAC, Lyric Theatre, Hammersmith and UK Tour), *Liza, Liza, Liza* (Tabard Theatre and UK Tour), *The Bridge* (Chelsea Theatre and Rose Theatre, Kingston), *Don't Exaggerate* (Jermyn Street Theatre), *SOLD* (Pleasance Edinburgh) and *The Good Actor* (Hoxton Hall). Associate Sound Design includes *You're A Good Man Charlie Brown* (Tabard Theatre).

Composition includes the trailer of Jonathan Harvey's *Beautiful Thing, Page One Theatre's The Bridge* and Underscore for *Made Up Stories from My Unmade Bed,* and Live Underscore for John Wight's *Divine Words.*

Live Sound Engineering includes work with the Duchess of Cambridge, David Cameron, Michael Caine, Boris Johnson, Professor Robert Winston, George Osborne and Michael Parkinson.

FINBOROUGH | THEATRE
VIBRANT **NEW WRITING** | UNIQUE **REDISCOVERIES**

"A disproportionately valuable
component of the London
theatre ecology. Its programme
combines new writing
and revivals, in selections
intelligent and audacious."
Financial Times

"The tiny but mighty
Finborough...one of the best
batting averages of any London
company." Ben Brantley,
The New York Times

"The Finborough Theatre, under
the artistic direction of Neil
McPherson, has been earning
a place on the must-visit
list with its eclectic, smartly
curated slate of new works and
neglected masterpieces." *Vogue*

Founded in 1980, the multi-award-winning Finborough Theatre
presents plays and music theatre, concentrated exclusively on
vibrant new writing and unique rediscoveries from the 19th and
20th centuries. Behind the scenes, we continue to discover and
develop a new generation of theatre makers – through our literary
team, and our programmes for both interns and Resident Assistant
Directors.

Despite remaining completely unsubsidised, the Finborough Theatre
has an unparalleled track record of attracting the finest creative
talent who go on to become leading voices in British theatre.
Under Artistic Director Neil McPherson, it has discovered some
of the UK's most exciting new playwrights including Laura Wade,
James Graham, Mike Bartlett, Sarah Grochala, Jack Thorne, Simon
Vinnicombe, Alexandra Wood, Al Smith, Nicholas de Jongh and
Anders Lustgarten; and directors including Blanche McIntyre.

Artists working at the theatre in the 1980s included Clive Barker, Rory Bremner, Nica Burns, Kathy Burke, Ken Campbell, Jane Horrocks and Claire Dowie. In the 1990s, the Finborough Theatre first became known for new writing including Naomi Wallace's first play *The War Boys*; Rachel Weisz in David Farr's *Neville Southall's Washbag*; four plays by Anthony Neilson including *Penetrator* and *The Censor*, both of which transferred to the Royal Court Theatre; and new plays by Richard Bean, Lucinda Coxon, David Eldridge, Tony Marchant and Mark Ravenhill. New writing development included the premieres of modern classics such as Mark Ravenhill's *Shopping and F***king*, Conor McPherson's *This Lime Tree Bower*, Naomi Wallace's *Slaughter City* and Martin McDonagh's *The Pillowman*.

Since 2000, new British plays have included Laura Wade's London debut *Young Emma*, commissioned for the Finborough Theatre; two one-woman shows by Miranda Hart; James Graham's *Albert's Boy* with Victor Spinetti; Sarah Grochala's *S27*; Peter Nichols' *Lingua Franca*, which transferred Off-Broadway; and West End transfers for Joy Wilkinson's *Fair*; Nicholas de Jongh's *Plague Over England*; and Jack Thorne's *Fanny and Faggot*. The late Miriam Karlin made her last stage appearance in *Many Roads to Paradise* in 2008. We have also produced our annual festival of new writing – *Vibrant – A Festival of Finborough Playwrights* annually since 2009.
UK premieres of foreign plays have included plays by Brad Fraser, Lanford Wilson, Larry Kramer, Tennessee Williams; the English premiere of Robert McLellan's Scots language classic, *Jamie the Saxt*; and three West End transfers – Frank McGuinness's *Gates of Gold* with William Gaunt and John Bennett; Joe DiPietro's *F***ing Men*; and Craig Higginson's *Dream of the Dog* with Dame Janet Suzman.

Rediscoveries of neglected work – most commissioned by the Finborough Theatre – have included the first London revivals of Rolf Hochhuth's *Soldiers* and *The Representative*; both parts of Keith Dewhurst's *Lark Rise to Candleford*; *The Women's War*, an evening of original suffragette plays; *Etta Jenks* with Clarke Peters and Daniela Nardini; Noël Coward's first play, *The Rat Trap*; Charles Wood's *Jingo* with Susannah Harker; Emlyn Williams' *Accolade*; Lennox Robinson's *Drama at Inish* with Celia Imrie and Paul O'Grady; John Van Druten's *London Wall* which transferred to St James' Theatre; and J. B. Priestley's *Cornelius*, which transferred to a sell out Off-Broadway run in New York City.

Music theatre has included the new (premieres from Grant Olding, Charles Miller, Michael John LaChuisa, Adam Guettel, Andrew Lippa,

Paul Scott Goodman, and Adam Gwon's *Ordinary Days* which transferred to the West End) and the old (the UK premiere of Rodgers and Hammerstein's *State Fair* which also transferred to the West End), and the acclaimed 'Celebrating British Music Theatre' series, reviving forgotten British musicals.

The Finborough Theatre won The Stage Fringe Theatre of the Year Award in 2011, *London Theatre Reviews'* Empty Space Peter Brook Award in 2010 and 2012, the Empty Space Peter Brook Award's Dan Crawford Pub Theatre Award in 2005 and 2008, the Empty Space Peter Brook Mark Marvin Award in 2004, and swept the board with eight awards at the 2012 OffWestEnd Awards including Best Artistic Director and Best Director for the second year running. *Accolade* was named Best Fringe Show of 2011 by *Time Out*. It is the only unsubsidised theatre ever to be awarded the Pearson Playwriting Award (now the Channel 4 Playwrights Scheme) nine times. Three bursary holders (Laura Wade, James Graham and Anders Lustgarten) have also won the Catherine Johnson Award for Pearson Best Play.

www.finboroughtheatre.co.uk

Our patrons are respectfully reminded that, in this intimate theatre, any noise such as rustling programmes, talking or the ringing of mobile phones may distract the actors and your fellow audience members. We regret there is no admittance or re-admittance to the auditorium whilst the performance is in progress.

FINBOROUGH | THEATRE

VIBRANT **NEW WRITING** | UNIQUE **REDISCOVERIES**
118 Finborough Road, London SW10 9ED
admin@finboroughtheatre.co.uk
www.finboroughtheatre.co.uk

The Finborough Theatre is a member of the Independent Theatre Council, the Society of Independent Theatres, Musical Theatre Network, The Friends of Brompton Cemetery and The Earl's Court Society
www.earlscourtsociety.org.uk

Supported by

Mailing
Email admin@finboroughtheatre.co.uk or give your details to our Box Office staff to join our free email list. If you would like to be sent a free season leaflet every three months, just include your postal address and postcode.

Feedback
We welcome your comments, complaints and suggestions. Write to Finborough Theatre, 118 Finborough Road, London SW10 9ED or email us at admin@finboroughtheatre.co.uk

Playscripts
Many of the Finborough Theatre's plays have been published and are on sale from our website.

Finborough Theatre T-Shirts
Finborough Theatre T-Shirts are on sale from the Box Office.

On social media

 www.facebook.com/FinboroughTheatre

 www.twitter.com/finborough

Friends
The Finborough Theatre is a registered charity. We receive no public funding, and rely solely on the support of our audiences. Please do consider supporting us by becoming a member of our Friends of the Finborough Theatre scheme. There are four categories of Friends, each offering a wide range of benefits.

Richard Tauber Friends – Val Bond. James Brown. Tom Erhardt. Stephen and Jennifer Harper. Richard Jackson. Mike Lewendon. John Lawson. Harry MacAuslan. Mark and Susan Nichols. Sarah Thomas. Kathryn McDowall. Barry Serjent. Lavinia Webb. Stephen Winningham.
Lionel Monckton Friends – Philip G Hooker. Martin and Wendy Kramer. Deborah Milner. Maxine and Eric Reynolds.
William Terriss Friends – Stuart Ffoulkes. Leo and Janet Liebster. Paul and Lindsay Kennedy. Corinne Rooney. Jon and NoraLee Sedmak.

Smoking is not permitted in the auditorium and the use of cameras and recording equipment is strictly prohibited.

In accordance with the requirements of the Royal Borough of Kensington and Chelsea:
1. The public may leave at the end of the performance by all doors and such doors must at that time be kept open.
2. All gangways, corridors, staircases and external passageways intended for exit shall be left entirely free from obstruction whether permanent or temporary.
3. Persons shall not be permitted to stand or sit in any of the gangways intercepting the seating or to sit in any of the other gangways.

The Finborough Theatre is licensed by the Royal Borough of Kensington and Chelsea to The Steam Industry, a registered charity and a company limited by guarantee. Registered in England and Wales no. 3448268. Registered Charity no. 1071304. Registered Office: 118 Finborough Road, London SW10 9ED.
The Steam Industry is under the overall Artistic Direction of Phil Willmott. www.philwillmott.co.uk

A MUSICAL

Book & Lyrics
PHIL WILLMOTT

Music
PHIL WILLMOTT
MARK COLLINS

WWW.SAMUELFRENCH.CO.UK
WWW.SAMUELFRENCH.COM

ISBN 978-0-573-18003-3

www.samuelfrench-london.co.uk

www.samuelfrench.com

FOR AMATEUR PRODUCTION ENQUIRIES

UNITED KINGDOM AND WORLD EXCLUDING NORTH AMERICA
plays@SamuelFrench-London.co.uk
020 7255 4302/01

UNITED STATES AND CANADA
info@SamuelFrench.com
1-866-598-8449

Each title is subject to availability from Samuel French,
depending upon country of performance.

Author's note
The history of Princess Caraboo and a musical

Around 1820 an aristocratic couple took a homeless girl under their wings having been convinced by a Spanish sailor and her unusual behaviour that she was an exotic princess, captured by pirates and shipwrecked in Britain without a word of English.

As news spread, her great beauty and the appeal of her story attracted much attention from powerful admirers and language experts keen to make their name by identifying her native tongue. She became a celebrity, was wined and dined in high society and a portrait was made for publication in *The Times*. This, however, proved her downfall when a couple recognised her as their run-away maid and she was unmasked as a fake, fleeing to America.

Nearly two centuries later I was commissioned by Tom Morris, the Artistic Director of the Bristol Old Vic, to write and direct a big, populist musical of sufficient scale to premiere at the venue or the vast Bristol Hippodrome. I decided to take the Princess Caraboo scandal as my subject.

I teamed up with the musical arranger, Mark Collins, who had impressed me as the Assistant Musical Director on another of my shows, Once Upon a Time at the Adelphi, a commission from Liverpool Playhouse and performed as one of the centrepieces of the city's year as European Capital of Culture. I wrote a script and lyrics for Princess Caraboo dictating melodies which Mark transcribed, arranged and augmented to create a score; a working method we've replicated on several commissions since.

When I considered how best to tell the story it was clear that an eleventh-hour exposure of the fake couldn't be the basis of the show as the audience would take their seats already knowing the truth. There was also little to be gained by exploring why "Caraboo" behaved as she did, this was pretty obvious as in those days arrest for vagrancy would result in flogging, transportation or even hanging. She grasped at the opportunity to escape punishment.

It was how the lies escalated and the circumstances and social conditions under which this could happen which began to fascinate me. The new vogue for exotica, following the re-establishment of international trade at the end of the Napoleonic War was undoubtedly a factor, as was a lack of understanding regarding anything "foreign" and the emotional vulnerability of her hosts. Also the vested interest of the many "experts" who vouched for her and who'd face disgrace should the Caraboo phenomenon be exposed played a part. Her powerful admirers would also have looked pretty stupid if her true identity had been questioned. Fascinating though this all was it still didn't give me an emotional heart for the piece.

The troublesome portrait was painted by a young artist called Edward Bird. My starting point was to imagine an attraction between them which would lead to her confiding in him. My thinking was that the burden this placed on him, deciding whether to expose and destroy the woman he loved or say nothing and become implicated in the duping of his friends, could be a spine for the musical and an exploration of when, how and why lies snowball on this scale. It would also add romance to the mix.

Next I needed a holding form. I'd become very fond of the Worralls, the couple whose kind hearts and ignorance led them to believe they'd adopted a princess. I speculated that their subsequent humiliation might motivate Sir Charles Worrall to host a lecture on the case and the nature of lying, illustrated by dramatisations performed by his servants. His intellectual curiosity about modern thinking might also give me a cheeky excuse to draw on future musical theatre styles and not be confined to those of 1820.

To add extra conflict I invented an adversary for Edward, Lord Marlborough, whose robust manner and turns of phrase are based on the racy language employed by several Regency rakes in their letters and diaries.

The theatre then allocated me time with their Youth Theatre to explore which themes might chime with a contemporary audience.

Having combined everything into a first draft we assembled a cast in Bristol to test out the show by presenting a rough staging resulting from a week of exploration and rehearsals. We performed it twice in the theatre's paint shop then returned to London for a one-off presentation as part of Vibrant – A Festival of Finborough Playwrights.

The response was extremely positive and the cash-strapped Bristol Old Vic began searching for a co-producer to help shoulder the financial burden of staging a full production. The powerful Ambassadors Theatre Group came on board and plans were made for the show to open at the Bristol Hippodrome ahead of a number one national tour. I cancelled a production in Connecticut so this would be the world premiere. Five years passed in which the project was on and off, on and off and on and off until finally it was concluded that it was, after all, too risky to produce as envisaged.

Which takes us to now. Mark and I had remained fond of the piece and rather than consign it to a bottom draw we decided to give it one final hurrah, squeezing what was always conceived to be a large-scale show back into the Finborough, for a full production this April.

The great news is that it's already been picked up for publication and licensing by Samuel French who accepted it within days of my submitting it for consideration and before we've even opened.

Hopefully this will mean that the Finborough Production won't be its one and only outing and, who knows, one day it may even be performed on the scale for which it was conceived.

Phil Willmott
March 2016

CHARACTERS

13 Female / 10 Male

Sir Charles Worrall
(M 35 + Upper class. Paternal, kindly and practical. Adores his wife)

Lady Elizabeth Worrall
(F 35+ Upper class, a motherly, excitable romantic. Loves her husband)

Sarah (The Worrall's chambermaid)
Playing the Princess Caraboo
(F Early 20s. Princess Caraboo is apparently an exotic beauty, speaking no English, from a far-away kingdom but who will turn out to be a working class girl from Exeter)

Andrew (The Worall's groom)
Playing Edward (Eddie) Bird
(M early 20s, Edward is merchant class, likable and ambitious if a little earnest)

Matthew (The Worall's footman)
Playing Osvaldo Agathias
(M 20s/30s Osvaldo is swarthy, sly and ruthless)

Burrows (The Worrall's steward)
Playing Lord Marlborough
(M 20s/30s. Marlborough is upper class, a handsome insensitive bully)

Richard (The Worrall's second footman)
Playing Mr Igel
(M Any age,. Igel is Marlborough's language expert from Holland)

Betty (The Worrall's parlour maid)
(F Any age. An excitable and chaotic young women)

Mrs Catesby (The Worrall's cook)
(F Any age. Warm-hearted but can be quick tempered)

Hatty (The Worrall's kitchen maid)
(F Any age. Enthusiastic but always keen to be doing things properly)

Lady Bettina
(F Any age)

Lady Catherine
(F Any age)

Lady Harriett
(F Any age)

A reporter from *The Times*
(M Any age)

Sir Mulberry Slivitt
(M Any age)

William Pitt the Younger
(M Any age)

Meg, a tavern maid
(F Any age)

1st Gossip (F Any age)

2nd Gossip (F Any age)

3rd Gossip (F Any age)

Lord Marlborough's manservant
(M Any age)

American Custom's official
(M Any age)

Additional servants
Guests of the Worralls
Guests of Lord Marlborough
Gossips
Passengers for America

SETTING
England, 1820

For the production at the Finborough Theatre we dressed
the stage to resemble Sir Charles Worrall's study but with
a huge gilded mirror, apparently mottled antique glass,
covering the entire back wall. (It was in fact distressed
Perspex within a timber frame.)

Characters would catch their reflection in it as appropriate
to a musical about fake identity.

When lit a certain way it reflected the action giving an
added depth and grandeur to the larger-scale scene.

At other times you could see right through the glass to a
series of dolls houses and a wooden ship which, when lit
appropriately, indicated the location of each scene, eg.
there was a dolls house representing the Worralls home
which lit up during scenes there and another representing
Lord Marlborough's house. The presence of the dolls
houses also symbolised Lady Elizabeth Worrall's mourning
for her daughter.

Sir Charles Worrall's desk was strong enough to stand on and
a low table close by served as a step up on to it. This gave us
two extra levels on which to play moments within crowded
scenes which required the audience's focus.

Scenes dovetailed with each other so that the action of each
half flowed continuously without a break in the rhythm.
Lighting changes differentiated locale and times of day
without the necessity for cumbersome scenery changes.

MUSICAL NUMBERS

ACT ONE

Overture

Bring on the 1820:	The Woralls and company
Shipwreck 1:	Osvaldo Agathias
Shipwreck 2:	Betty, Hatty, Richard and Mrs Catesby
Home:	Eddie with Betty, Hatty, Richard and Mrs Catesby
Salam:	Eddie, Sir Charles Worrall, Lady Elizabeth Worrall with Betty, Hatty, Richard and Mrs Catesby
Speaking Caraboo:	Mr Igel, Princess Caraboo and Company *
Lullaby:	Princess Caraboo
Wait!:	Eddie
Just Say Yes:	Lord Marlborough and Company
I am my Own Person:	Princess Caraboo

ACT TWO

Entr'acte

Truth:	Company *
A Portrait of the Princess Caraboo:	Eddie
Understanding:	Eddie and Princess Caraboo with Betty, Hatty, and Mrs Catesby
When:	Osvaldo Agathias
Fabulous:	Eddie, Princess Caraboo, Lord Marlborough, The Worralls and Company *
Bad News:	Osvaldo Agathias, Betty, Hatty, Richard, Mrs Catesby and the Company *
Without Your Love:	Princess Caraboo
Daughters:	Lady Elizabeth Worrall and Princess Caraboo
The Wedding of the Princess Caraboo:	Sir Charles Worrall, Eddie, Betty, Hatty, Richard and Mrs Catesby
Conclusions:	Company
Bows and Finale:	The Company *

* Dance numbers

ACT ONE

Overture

SIR CHARLES WORRALL *in a spotlight.*

He is an affable man of 35+.

SIR CHARLES WORRALL *(to the audience)* Good evening, everyone and welcome to Briarwood Hall.

When I announced my little talk on the study of lies and lying, in particular the Princess Caraboo scandal to which I was, of course, an unwitting party, the response was so great I thought it prudent to abandon the lecture room at the Royal Society and invite you here, to my home; the scene of several of the more infamous incidents.

My dear wife, who was herself caught up in events, and my servants, many of whom served the Princess personally have striven to recreate a number of dramatic tableaux, in a variety of modern musical theatre styles, with which to bring the story to life.

Our musical accompaniment this evening will be provided by fellow parishioners. *(Referring to the modern keyboard)* Led by the vicar on the latest addition to his collection of clockwork musical automata, which I won't pretend to understand.

Yes indeed, ours is truly a time of enlightenment and new influences from across our colonies.

This is the world into which Princess Caraboo sprang
so readily to life.

He sings.

"THE 1820S"

NAPOLEON SITS BROKEN ON SOME ISLAND.
THAT TYRANT WHO WOULD CRUSH US ROARS NO MORE.
RIGHT ACROSS THE GLOBE THEY CHEER OUR VICT'RY
AND SEND THEIR GOODS AND PEOPLE TO OUR SHORE.
SOON ENGLAND WILL BE HOST TO THE EXOTIC.
QUIXOTIC WONDERS CROSS THE SEVEN SEAS.
A WORLD OF THINGS WHICH WE JUST CAN'T IMAGINE
WILL FIND THEIR WAY TO HARBOURS SUCH AS THESE.

THIS IS THE 1820S
DARE TO DREAM ONCE MORE
EMBRACE THE 1820S
LET YOUR MIND EXPLORE.

THERE'LL BE A NATIVE PAINTING
HANGING OVER EVERYBODY'S HEARTH.
WE CAN RIDE AN ELEPHANT
AND MAKE A FRIEND OF A GIRAFFE.
WE'LL SIT ON PERSIAN MATTING
EFFORTLESSLY CHATTING
IN WALLOON
SPARRING WITH A TSAR OR A PASSING
FARSI OF RANGOON.

(spoken summoning the servants to the stage) Servants, if
you please!

The household assemble and join in.

ALL

WE'LL BE TAUGHT TO RECOGNISE
STRANGE DIALECTS AND TERMS
LEARN NEW NAMES OF ANIMALS AND BIRDS.

MRS CATESBY

THERE'LL BE FOREIGN FOWL TO COOK

I CAN'T EVEN PRONOUNCE.

RICHARD

WE'LL LEARN NEW EXOTIC DIRTY WORDS!

EVERYONE *(spoken)* Richard! etc

BETTY

I'LL HAVE TO START PARTING MY LADY'S HAIR
LIKE FOREIGN HEADS.

MATTHEW

MASTER'S BOUND TO BORE ON 'BOUT
EACH FOREIGN MORON THAT HE'S READ.

HATTY

THERE WILL BE NEW DISEASES,
FOREIGN COUGHS AND SNEEZES,
WE SHOULD DREAD.

MRS CATESBY

WELL, I FOR ONE, THINK THAT WE'LL
ALL BE MURDERED IN OUR BEDS!

SIR CHARLES WORRALL *(correcting them)*

THIS IS THE 1820S
DARE TO DREAM ONCE MORE
EMBRACE THE 1820S
LET YOUR MIND EXPLORE.

(spoken to the audience) Ladies and gentlemen, may I
present my good lady wife.

LADY ELIZABETH WORRALL *enters.*

LADY ELIZABETH WORRALL

ISN'T THIS EXCITING EV'RYBODY?
WHAT A WORLD!
SO FULL OF OPPORTUNITIES TO SEIZE!

BURROWS

THERE'S RUMOURS 'BOUT A REVOLUTION
ON THE STREETS OF FRANCE.

LADY ELIZABETH WORRALL *(curbing him)*

WE'LL HAVE NO MORE OF THAT TALK

IF YOU PLEASE!

ALL

THERE'LL BE A NATIVE PAINTING
HANGING OVER EVERBODY'S HEARTH.
WE CAN RIDE AN ELEPHANT
AN' MAKE A FRIEND OF A GIRAFFE.
IT'S THE TIME FOR TRADING,
AN' NO LONGER RAIDING
BONAPARTE.

Big finish.

NO USE IN WORRYING
"WHAT WILL THE FUTURE BRING?"
IT'S TIME TO LET THE 1820S START!

Everyone is very pleased with the opening number!

LADY ELIZABETH WORRALL Well done, well done everybody!
Splendid, splendid! *(presenting them for applause)* The
servants everyone! Everything you'll see this evening
has been willingly rehearsed during their half-days off
with not a grumble.

*The servants look shifty as if this weren't entirely the
case.*

SIR CHARLES WORRALL Right, places everybody for scene
two. It is time to meet our princess or rather a dramatic
re-creation of how we first made her acquaintance.

The bustle of people clearing but **LADY ELIZABETH
WORRALL** *stands transfixed as if in thought.*

(gently sugesting she should leave the stage) My dear…

LADY ELIZABETH WORRALL Oh, my love I can't help
thinking –

SIR CHARLES WORRALL Yes, my dove, I know what you're
thinking.

LADY ELIZABETH WORRALL How she would have loved…

SIR CHARLES WORRALL Yes, now we've talked about this haven't we? *(indicating the audience)* Our esteemed guests are waiting.

LADY ELIZABETH WORRALL *(brightening and focussed again)* Oh, yes of course. Is it…?

SIR CHARLES WORRALL It's the storm scene.

LADY ELIZABETH WORRALL Oh I do love this one. *(To the audience)* Now I think you'll enjoy this. *(Introducing the servant cast member)* Sarah here will be taking the role of the princess.

SIR CHARLES WORRALL *(to SARAH)* Now remember my dear, no embellishments. The incident just as you observed it if you please.

SARAH *curtsies.*

LADY ELIZABETH WORRALL Matthew will be taking the role of the scurrilous foreign sailor.

MATTHEW *(to the audience)* I played Lucifer in the pageant last Easter.

SIR CHARLES WORRALL Any chance of a little more restraint, tonight?

MATTHEW Absolutely none, your lordship.

SIR CHARLES WORRALL Heaven help us.

LADY ELIZABETH WORRALL And Burrows will play our night watchman.

BURROWS I am your night watchman, your Ladyship.

LADY ELIZABETH WORRALL Ah, yes of course. Well, that shouldn't be much of a challenge then. Chop, chop everyone.

The stage empties except for **SIR CHARLES WORRALL**.

SIR CHARLES WORRALL Everybody ready?

ALL *(from off)* Yes.

Lullaby underscoring.

SIR CHARLES WORRALL The ancient Greek philosopher
Aracticus writing in the early third century BC was
much concerned with the nature of liars and the act
of lying. From the great library at Alexandria he draws
a correlation between upset of the natural order and
deviation from commonly held notions of truth. So to
introduce our title character we have, appropriately
enough, the wildest storm this parish has ever seen.
Pray: do not be alarmed by the stage effects. Our
underfootman are preparing to roll a cannonball
along the corridor above us as we distil our candle
light via shutters and muslin. We begin. The great
storm!

*Thunder and lightning. The servant actors become
completely submerged in their roles.*

BURROWS, *the night watchman leads on a wretched and
bedraggled* **OSVALDO AGATHIAS**, *who is an accented,
charasmatic con-man, and the beautiful* "**PRINCESS
CARABOO** ".

OSVALDO AGATHIAS *(to* **BURROWS***)* Be careful who you
push around, peasant. You will die of shame when the
story of this night is told.

BURROWS You'll be quiet, if you don't want another clout.
I've had just about enough of you. Sir Charles will get
to the bottom of this.

SIR CHARLES WORRALL *enters with* **RICHARD**, *the
footman.*

SIR CHARLES WORRALL What on earth is it, Burrows?

BURROWS We found a couple of itinerants begging outside
the gate.

SIR CHARLES WORRALL Well, lock them up, can't you? I'm quite sure this could have waited until the morning.

BURROWS Sorry, I did but…your lordship it's just the girl's sick, I'm not sure she'll last the night and well, in the circumstances, I thought you'd want to hear this. *(shoves* **OSVALDO AGATHIAS** *forward)* Tell his lordship what you told me.

OSVALDO AGATHIAS Greetings of the night to you, most honoured Sir. I am Osvaldo Agathias at your service!

BURROWS *(wacks him)* None of your guff now, just tell it straight.

SIR CHARLES WORRALL Thank you Burrows, let the fellow speak.

   LADY ELIZABETH WORRALL *enters with* **BETTY**.

LADY ELIZABETH WORRALL Charles! Charles! What's going on?

OSVALDO AGATHIAS   *(to* **LADY ELIZABETH WORRALL***)* Honoured and most beautiful lady!

LADY ELIZABETH WORRALL Oh!

SIR CHARLES WORRALL Go back to your needlepoint, my love. It's just parish business.

LADY ELIZABETH WORRALL Can we get this poor girl a chair, she looks as if she's about to faint? Are we barbarians Charles?

SIR CHARLES WORRALL No, no of course not. Richard, a chair for the girl.

   It's brought by **RICHARD** *and* **PRINCESS CARABOO** *sits.*

LADY ELIZABETH WORRALL Are you alright, my dear?

OSVALDO AGATHIAS Alas, Ladyship she does not speak English. But I can tell you she faints with hunger and homesickness for the royal court of Carabatta.

LADY ELIZABETH WORRALL *(to* **RICHARD***)* Tell Mrs Catesby to see a fortifying supper is prepared.

SIR CHARLES WORRALL Now, my dear, I'm sure you need not concern yourself.

BURROWS It's a matter for the magistrate, your Ladyship.

LADY ELIZABETH WORRALL You men are such brutes it's clear what this girl needs is a mother's compassion.

SIR CHARLES WORRALL Shall we hear what the foreigner has to say my love, before we jump to any conclusions? There are legal processes…

LADY ELIZABETH WORRALL Then get on with it Charles, the sooner this poor waif has a hot meal and a bed for the night the better.

OSVALDO AGATHIAS Ah, Ladyship it is clear you have the finer sentiments which recognise royalty in peril.

LADY ELIZABETH WORRALL Royalty?

BURROWS I've warned you. We just want your story, nothing else.

OSVALDO AGATHIAS Very well, the story of Princess Caraboo. I have but the slightest fragments of her mother tongue but this is what I've been able to piece together.

"THE SHIPWRECK 1"

SHE COMES FROM
FAR AWAY FROM HERE
AN ISLAND IN A GLITTERING SEA,
SHE WAS BORN IN A PALACE
TO A KING AND QUEEN
AND LIVED HER LIFE IN LUXURY.

THEN PIRATES STORMED THE ISLE
AND SOUGHT TO RIP

HER FROM HER PARENTS FOR THEIR PIRATE SHIP
THE BRIGANDS USED HER ROUGHLY
THINKING NO DOUBT THEY COULD MESH
A FORTUNE, FOR THEIR SLAVE IN MARAKESH.

LADY ELIZABETH WORRALL *(spoken. In alarm)* Charles!

OSVALDO AGATHIAS

BUT FORTUNE HAD ANOTHER FATE IN MIND
A FURTHER BLOW OR MAYBE IT WAS KIND
ANYWAY A TEMPEST CAUSED THE BRIGANDS' SHIP TO VEER
TILL THEY WERE SHIPWRECKED BUT A MILE FROM HERE.

AT A PORT CLOSE BY
MY FRIENDS AND I
OBSERVED THE SAILORS' PLIGHT
SAINT CHRISTOPHER, OUR PATRON SAINT
WOULD GUIDE OUR HAND THAT NIGHT.

I HELPED HER FROM THE FREEZING TIDE
I BROUGHT HER HERE, WHERE YOU RESIDE.

AND SO I PRAY, YOU WON'T TURN US AWAY
THE WEATHER'S CRUEL, SHE HAS NO PLACE TO STAY
I HUMBLY BEG, MOST HONOURED SIR, TO INTRODUCE TO
    YOU
HER ROYAL HIGHNESS, PRINCESS CARABOO.

BURROWS I've heard some tall tales from vagrants facing a flogging but I thought your Honour might want to hear this lot. Especially since *(cynically indicating the princess)* "Her Royal Highness" here looks about to drop dead.

LADY ELIZABETH WORRALL Thank heavens you brought her to us.

SIR CHARLES WORRALL Now, my dear. Let us not jump to hasty conclusions. As Burrows says –

LADY ELIZABETH WORRALL I don't care what Burrows says, and neither should you, a young girl is dying and providence has delivered her to our door. You of all people should see the significance. It's a sign.

SIR CHARLES WORRALL Oh, now, my dear, you must not let your kind heart blind you to the fact –

LADY ELIZABETH WORRALL Nonsense, I can see God's mercy even if you pretend you can't. I won't hear another word about it. She's to be nursed back to strength and this man (**OSVALDO AGATHIAS**) will be suitably accommodated until he can translate her full story.

BURROWS There's plenty in the gaol house speak fluent hog-wash.

SIR CHARLES WORRALL Yes, thank you. Burrows, you may go now. The prisone – I mean, our guests will be provided for as my wife suggests. Betty, make up the Chinese room for the prin – for the girl.

BETTY Yes, my lord.

MRS CATESBY *storms in and overhears* –

SIR CHARLES WORRALL And Richard, put the foreign gentleman in the stable block.

RICHARD Yes, my lord.

OSVALDO AGATHIAS Most kind, lordship. Most kind!

BETTY *shows* **PRINCESS CARABOO** *out,* **RICHARD** *does the same with* **OSVALDO AGATHIAS**.

MRS CATESBY Sir Charles, your Ladyship. Is it true I'm expected to feed a filthy beggar girl off the street, in my kitchen?

LADY ELIZABETH WORRALL If you would, Mrs Catesby. A clear broth should suffice, we do not know what her delicate stomach is used to.

MRS CATESBY *(indicating* **OSVALDO AGATHIAS**'s *direction)* What about 'im?

LADY ELIZABETH WORRALL Could you rustle up a little supper with a Spanish bent?

MRS CATESBY I most certainly could not! I'm a respectable Christian woman! I've just boiled up some sheep's eyes for the dogs; he can have a bowl of that and think himself lucky.

SIR CHARLES WORRALL Mrs C, you are, as ever, a marvel.

THE WORALLS *and* **MRS CATESBY** *exit.*

HATTY *and* **BETTY** *return and sing –*

"THE SHIPWRECK" – Reprise

HATTY

AND SO IT WAS, THAT DARK AND STORMY NIGHT
THE MASTER AND THE MISTRESS HEARD HER PLIGHT.

BETTY

WHAT HAPPENED NEXT, IT'S HARD TO SAY
JUST WHO WAS WRONG OR RIGHT.

BOTH

THAT DARK AND STORMY, WRETCHED, CRU-EL NIGHT.

MRS CATESBY *and* **RICHARD** *returns.*

MRS CATESBY

THE SPANNIARD, HUNKERED DOWN AND ATE HIS FILL
BUT SHE TOUCHED NOTHING, SITTING, PALE AND ILL.

RICHARD

TWO HOURS LATER, CALM RESTORED,
THE HOUSE LAY DARK AND STILL
NO SIGN OF TROUBLE, WELL, OF COURSE UNTIL –

A shot is heard. **BURROWS** *runs on with a blunderbuss.*

THE WORRALLS *rush on again.*

BURROWS I caught them red-handed, sir! Foreign – royalty, my arse.

SIR CHARLES WORRALL What on earth...?

> **OSVALDO AGATHIAS** *drags* **PRINCESS CARABOO** *on, with a knife to her throat and a hand over her mouth.*

OSVALDO AGATHIAS Another move and I slit her throat!

LADY ELIZABETH WORRALL Charles!

SIR CHARLES WORRALL Unhand that girl at once!

OSVALDO AGATHIAS Not likely, she's my ticket out of here!

> *He drags her accross the stage. Silverware falls from his pocket in the struggle.* **BURROWS** *relaods the gun.*

LADY ELIZABETH WORRALL Charles! The silverware!

SIR CHARLES WORRALL What the –

> **PRINCESS CARABOO** *collapses in a faint, slipping from* **OSVALDO AGATHIAS**'s *arms to the floor.*

> *The* **WORRALLS** *and servants rush to her,* **OSVALDO AGATHIAS** *runs off,* **BURROWS** *fires another shot after him.*

BURROWS It's too dark, I'm sorry your lordship. *(Indicating* **PRINCESS CARABOO**) Least we've got one of 'em.

LADY ELIZABETH WORRALL *(cradling* **PRINCESS CARABOO**) Oh, my dear. That fiend. To try to kidnap you. After all you've endured. Do not worry, you're safe now. You're home.

BURROWS But your Ladyship...

SIR CHARLES WORRALL That's enough Burrows. To bed everyone!

> *Servants drift away back to bed.*

Music – lullaby underscoring.

LADY ELIZABETH WORRALL I will sit up with her, Charles.

SIR CHARLES WORRALL I beg of you my dear, do not invest too much in the girl, after all we've yet to ascertain if –

LADY ELIZABETH WORRALL I will not be contradicted in this, Charles. I have not forgotten a mother's compassion. Is it so long since you thought as a father?

SIR CHARLES WORRALL My love – that is unfair.

LADY ELIZABETH WORRALL I shall nurse her, at least through the night. Let that be an end of it.

She exits.

Lights restore to normal.

SIR CHARLES WORRALL A stormy night! A staple background to immoral acts, from the plays of Shakespeare to the Gothic novella. As Aracticus philosophised many centuries ago, social order and the natural order are inextricably linked. *(Beat)* And now it is time to introduce our second major character in this ignoble history.

LADY ELIZABETH WORRALL *enters brightly.*

LADY ELIZABETH WORRALL The love interest.

SIR CHARLES WORRALL Yes, my dear but do keep in mind this is a scientific lecture. We are not at home to Miss Austen's fascination with the heart.

LADY ELIZABETH WORRALL And yet our hearts played a role.

SIR CHARLES WORRALL Indeed they did.

LADY ELIZABETH WORRALL *(to the audience)* Lovely, lovely Edward. Our godson. Now Edward will be played by Andrew our groom. That terrible night Edward's own ship was struggling to harbour. He had not seen his home town for ten years. Imagine how his breast swelled with mixed emotion as the gales subsided and our coast came into view.

SIR CHARLES WORRALL   Yes, my dear. Andrew has been well briefed. I think we can rely on him to convey the moment.

LADY ELIZABETH WORRALL   Oh yes, yes. Of course. God speed Edward! I mean good luck Andrew.

THE WORRALLS *leave the stage and* **EDDIE** *is on the deck of a ship.*

He sings –

"HOME"

EDDIE

I OUGHT TO REST, THE VOYAGE WAS A TORTURE HOUSE OF PAIN.
FREEZING QUARTERS, CRAMPED CONDITIONS, COLD RELENTLESS RAIN.
BUT YET AT ANY MOMENT DAWN'LL BREAK ON MY HOME TOWN.
I WOULDN'T MISS IT FOR THE EARTH,
THAT FIRST SIGHT OF MY PLACE OF BIRTH.
THE SMELL OF IT, THE TASTE OF IT
I'M HOME.

HOME, HOME
IT'S TIME TO DO MY DUTY NOW
AND TAKE THE HOMEWARD TRACK
HOME, HOME
COULDN'T WAIT TO SPREAD MY WINGS AND LEAVE,
BUT NOW IT'S CALLED ME BACK!

EDDIE *disembarks.*

SHOULDN'T HOME BE TRIMMED WITH MIGHTY TOWERS?
STREETS OF PLENTY STREWN WITH PRETTY FLOWERS?
I'VE SEEN MEN REDUCED TO TEARS
RECALLING HOW HE'D DWELL
IN SOME LOST SUNLIT PARADISE.

WHO'D MISS THIS GRIMY HELL?

HOME, HOME...
IT'S TIME TO DO MY DUTY NOW
AND TAKE THE HOMEWARD TRACK
HOME, HOME
COULDN'T WAIT TO SPREAD MY WINGS AND LEAVE,
BUT NOW IT'S CALLED ME BACK!

RICHARD *arrives from the Worrall house.*

RICHARD Master Edward, Master Edward. Welcome home, I'm sorry to rush you, with you just arriving and all but Sir Charles would like to see you. At your earliest convenience, he says.

EDDIE Great heavens, perhaps Father left even more debt then I imagined.

RICHARD It's not that, it's a translation he's after.

EDDIE I'm afraid my Latin's a little rusty these days, Richard.

RICHARD It isn't Latin he's needing. It's something more rare. It's hard to know what language...you'd best come to the Hall. Her Ladyship will tell you all about it!

EDDIE Do tell your master and mistress I'll be there directly.

RICHARD Very good, sir. And, truly, welcome home.

RICHARD *exits.*

EDDIE

IF ONLY THINGS HAD STAYED THE WAY I LEFT THEM.
WHO FORESAW MY TROUBLED FATHER'S DEATH, THEN?
HE WROTE MY LEAVING BROKE HIS HEART
IT SEEMS NOW THAT WAS TRUE.
PA, I'D GIVE SO MANY THINGS
TO THROW MY ARMS ROUND YOU.

ENSEMBLE Home, home *(harmonies underneath).*

EDDIE

> BUT HOME MOVES ON AND SO MUST I
> I BEAR THE FAMILY NAME, I'LL TRY
> TO BE A BETTER FELLOW THEN MY FATHER WAS
> AND BUILD MYSELF A HOME.
>
> HE DIED IN DEBT, SOME SAY A LIAR
> BUT HE GAVE US ALL A ROOF AND FIRE.
> AND WHEN I'VE CHILDREN OF MY OWN
> THEY TOO WILL CALL THIS HOME.

> *Reaching* **THE WORRALL**'s *home he's greeted by* **BURROWS, RICHARD, HATTY, BETTY** *and* **MRS CATESBY**.

BETTY

> WELL BLESS ME LOOK WHO'S HOME!

EDDIE

> BETTY!

HATTY

> THE PRODIGAL'S COME HOME.

EDDIE

> HATTY!

MRS CATESBY

> SO FINALLY YOU'RE HOME.

EDDIE

> I'VE LOST THE URGE TO ROAM (**MRS C**)
> I'M HOME!

ALL

> WELCOME HOME!

MRS CATESBY Hurry, they're waiting for you upstairs.

> **SIR CHARLES WORRALL** *in a spotlight.*

SIR CHARLES WORRALL Aracticus identifies what he calls the Calpernian moment in the evolution of the

Alphanus Moratus, or the "Great Lie" if you will. This is the moment when corroboration by an authoritative outsider gives the deception an added credence allowing the falsehood to flourish. Aracticus is at pains to point out that this third party is often completely unaware that voicing, what is for them, an honest opinion is inadvertently fuelling a powerful deception.

The **WORRALL**'*s drawing room.*

The couple greet **EDDIE** *enthusiastically.*

HATTY *and* **BETTY** *stand in attendance.*

LADY ELIZABETH WORRALL Oh Edward, look at you, all grown up. Your poor father would have been so proud.

EDDIE Thank you your Ladyship.

SIR CHARLES WORRALL Welcome back Edward.

EDDIE Thank you, sir.

LADY ELIZABETH WORRALL Can we get you some refreshment? We want to hear about all your travels.

SIR CHARLES WORRALL The Barberry was it? The Indies? China we heard.

EDDIE Well...certainly.

LADY ELIZABETH WORRALL You were but a boy when you left us. Our darling girl had just been taken by the angels and I fear we did not take as much notice of your leave taking as we might. You had just turned eighteen I think.

EDDIE I had.

LADY ELIZABETH WORRALL And such a sweet, little thing.

EDDIE Let us pray that the world has made a man of me. Your Ladyship, I've taken the liberty of bringing you a silk shawl from the far China Seas. This one I feel is the perfect sapphire of your eyes.

LADY ELIZABETH WORRALL Edward you charmer. Thank you. You always know just the thing to say.

SIR CHARLES WORRALL Which brings us to our little problem...

LADY ELIZABETH WORRALL Yes, we need your help.

SIR CHARLES WORRALL You remember the storms of last week?

EDDIE Indeed I do. I was holed up at Calais.

SIR CHARLES WORRALL Well, it seems a young woman was kidnapped by pirates and shipwrecked near here, barely alive. She has nothing in her possession. A small piece of soap. A few pennies.

LADY ELIZABETH WORRALL But her hands, Charles. So smooth and delicate, unused to hard labour. *(Softly)* Like a doll.

SIR CHARLES WORRALL We sorely need the corroboration of one we can trust. Last assizes Justice Bartholomew sentenced a vagrant girl to hang.

LADY ELIZABETH WORRALL So you see it is most important that we find out the truth. "Caraboo". What language is that Edward? You have such a facility with foreign dialects.

SIR CHARLES WORRALL Carabatta must be a very small island. I cannot find reference to it.

EDDIE I...it's hard to say. Forgive me I cannot help but feel a certain scepticism. A foreign princess... Pirates.

BETTY When you meet her, Master Eddie...there's something about her.

HATTY She's not like folk around here.

   MRS CATESBY *arrives.*

MRS CATESBY I took her that Chinese tea you ordered, myself, Your Ladyship. She's a little more composed.

LADY ELIZABETH WORRALL This way Edward. You'll see it too. I know you will.

Lights change to gloom.

Everyone tentatively approaches **PRINCESS CARABOO**'s *room.*

EDDIE Why is it so dark in here?

LADY ELIZABETH WORRALL Open the curtains, Hatty.

MRS CATESBY She won't let me marm, she wants it this way. You know how particular she is with her tea.

We hear chanting from **PRINCESS CARABOO** *in the darkness. She's making up a sound which she believes sounds "foreign".*

EDDIE Your Ladyship?

LADY ELIZABETH WORRALL She will not drink from any cup until she has made such an incantation.

SIR CHARLES WORRALL She calls blessing on the vessel perhaps.

EDDIE Great heavens. I've encountered this before.

LADY ELIZABETH WORRALL Edward?

   "SALAM"

EDDIE *(sings)*
ON THE EASTERN COAST, OF THE CASPIAN SEA
THERE'S A PEOPLE HALF EGYPTIAN AND HALF TARTARY.
THEY BEGIN EACH MEAL THUS ASSIDUOUSLY.
COULD THIS HELP US SOLVE THE MYSTERY?

Vamp under –

SIR CHARLES WORRALL Egyptian you say? Is our guest perhaps a gypsy? *(Loudly and slowly to* **PRINCESS**

CARABOO) Do you have any lucky heather for us my dear?

LADY ELIZABETH WORRALL Charles, be quiet!

EDDIE This is no common traveller's incantation. *(To* **PRINCESS CARABOO**) Salam. *(no response)* Salam!

LADY ELIZABETH WORRALL What is the boy saying?

EDDIE Salam is the customary greeting in that part of the world.

LADY ELIZABETH WORRALL Oh I see.

EDDIE Salam

From the darkness.

PRINCESS CARABOO Salam

LADY ELIZABETH WORRALL Charles, Charles do you hear? She spoke to him! Ask her something else Edward. Ask her how she got here.

EDDIE *(sings)*
ALAS I'VE LITTLE KNOWLEDGE OF THE CASPIAN TONGUE
IT'S A LANGUAGE BARELY SPOKEN NOW BY ANYONE.
BUT THEIR CUSTOMARY CONDUCT,
THEIR SPIRIT AND VERVE,
I'VE BEEN LUCKY ENOUGH TO OBSERVE.

Vamp continues.

LADY ELIZABETH WORRALL Betty, the curtains!

Lights up on **PRINCESS CARABOO** *as* **BETTY** *arrears to open the curtains. She turns and* **EDDIE** *is face to face with her for the first time.*

1820s theme.

Vamp continues.

EDDIE *gives a little bow.*

PRINCESS CARABOO Salam.

She salams in return, using first one hand, then the other, then both.

LADY ELIZABETH WORRALL Edward, what do you conclude from the hand gestures?

EDDIE Rather inconclusive I'm afraid.

SIR CHARLES WORRALL Something of a false salam you might say.

LADY ELIZABETH WORRALL Charles!

EDDIE Have you an atlas Sir Charles?

SIR CHARLES WORRALL Hatty, fetch the large red book from the library, the one with the phases of the moon along the spine. And a pen and ink if you will, Betty. I feel we must record this extraordinary anthropological moment.

The maids exit.

EDDIE *(sings)*
HOME, HOME.
YET HERE'S AN EIGHTH NEW WONDER OF THE WORLD.
HOME, HOME,
A RICH SILK OF THE ORIENT UNFURLED.

Vamp continues.

The maids return with atlas etc.

(sings)

Salam tune.

FIND ME A PICTURE OF THE CASPIAN SEA.
CAN SHE POINT HER HOME OUT TO US ACCURATELY?

The atlas is held out to **PRINCESS CARABOO** *but she turns away.*

SIR CHARLES WORRALL *(sings)*
SHE LOOKS... WELL... CONFUSED AND ALARMED TO ME.

NOT THE AMAZON WE THOUGHT SHE WOULD BE.

Vamp continues.

LADY ELIZABETH WORRALL *(spoken)* Nonsense Charles. Name the three rivers that intertwine before Salisbury Cathedral but twenty miles from here.

SIR CHARLES WORRALL Well, I'd have to think about it.

LADY ELIZABETH WORRALL Exactly, all the girl's confusion demonstrates is that she has as little concept of geography as you do.

EDDIE Wait, I have an idea. Your Ladyship, that shawl I brought you, if I may. If you would be so kind to wear it thus and thus.

He arranges the shawl as an exotic headdress.

The ink please. I recall the queen mother has a birth mark in the shape of a crescent moon, considered a blessing from the gods and a sign of great beauty.

LADY ELIZABETH WORRALL You may anoint me Edward.

EDDIE *(hesitantly)* Alas her teeth are stained with beetle nut juice.

LADY ELIZABETH WORRALL Give me the ink,

She pretends to black out her teeth.

EDDIE *guides* **PRINCESS CARABOO** *around to face her.*

PRINCESS CARABOO *gasps and falls to her knees.*

EDDIE Your mother, yes?

PRINCESS CARABOO *(repeating the word as if new)* Mother!

EDDIE *takes* **SIR CHARLES WORRALL** *off.*

LADY ELIZABETH WORRALL *(sings)*
HOME, HOME.

YOU'VE FOUND A SECOND MOTHER, DEAR IN ME.
HOME, HOME.
TILL YOUR RETURN THIS HOUSE IS WHERE YOU'LL BE.

SIR CHARLES WORRALL *(from off)* Edward, is this fancy dress quite necessary? Elizabeth, really. I've a cushion on my head and a tablecloth for a cloak!

EDDIE *returns with* **SIR CHARLES WORRALL** *worrall done up in a home-made maharaja outfit as described.*

EDDIE *(sings)*

Coahing **SIR CHARLES WORRALL** *into role as* **PRINCESS CARABOO***'s Maharajah father.*

THE KING OF CARABBATTA HAS A BEVY OF SLAVES.

Music as **EDDIE** *organises the maids,* **RICHARD** *and* **MRS CATESBY** *to play exotic slave girls, surrounding* **SIR CHARLES WORRALL** *as the Maharajah.*

HE'S AS FAT AS ANY ELEPHANT
AND SCOWLS WHEN HE WAVES.

SIR CHARLES WORRALL *enacts this and* **PRINCESS CARABOO** *appears to recognise him as her father.*

(delighted sings)
HA HA! SHE SEES HER FATHER
IN THE WAY THAT YOU WAVED.

SIR CHARLES WORRALL *(sings)*
MY BOY IT SEEMS THE DAY IS SAVED!

ALL *(not* **PRINCESS CARABOO***)*
DID YOU EVER FIND A FAMILY AS HAPPY AS THIS?

SIR CHARLES WORRALL
AT LAST THE CHILD IS SMILING –

PRINCESS CARABOO *kisses* **MRS WORRALL.**

LADY ELIZABETH WORRALL

OH MY, CHARLES! A KISS!

EDDIE *bows before* **PRINCESS CARABOO**.

EDDIE
I REMAIN YOUR HUMBLE SERVANT.

She giggles.
NO, NO I INSIST.

ALL United in domestic bliss.

Musical vamp continues.

LADY ELIZABETH WORRALL What is your name child?

She points to herself.

Mother.

PRINCESS CARABOO *repeats.*

PRINCESS CARABOO Mother.

SIR CHARLES WORRALL Father.

PRINCESS CARABOO Father.

EDDIE Edward.

PRINCESS CARABOO *(pointing to herself)* Caraboo.

The English bow.

EDDIE AND THE WORRALLS Princess Caraboo!

LADY ELIZABETH WORRALL The whole county will want to meet her.

SIR CHARLES WORRALL And they shall. A ball I think, Elizabeth.

LADY ELIZABETH WORRALL Oh Charles, a ball? So many strangers may frighten her.

SIR CHARLES WORRALL Then the ladies, at least, will dress as she is accustomed. Edward, you will advise.

THE WORRALLS, EDDIE *and* **PRINCESS CARABOO** *leave.*

Lights change.

Vamp continues.

SIR CHARLES WORRALL *(to the audience)* The wily old philosopher correctly identifies the renewed commitment it requires to take a lie from the privacy of one's own home out into the world. For, in these circumstances, one can assume persons of substance are as gullible as one's servants.

The ball.

BETTY, HATTY *and* **MRS CATESBY** *become upper-class English women gathered for a ball in Arabic fancy dress.*

LADY CATHERINE (MRS CATESBY) My dears, don't we look quite the picture from the Arabian Nights?

LADY ELIZABETH WORRALL (BETTY) With but few words of English Princess Caraboo has quite conquered our entire little set.

LADY HARRIET (HATTY) I do adore a masquerade.

LADY ELIZABETH WORRALL Such silks, such colours!

LADY HARRIET It makes one wish one could dress like this always.

LADY CATHERINE It would quite enliven the Pump Room at Bath.

LADY ELIZABETH WORRALL But I fear young gallants would find it too frivolous.

LADY CATHERINE Nonsense my dear, they buzz around her like bees to honey.

ANNOUNCEMENT FROM OFFSTAGE Sir Mulberry Slivitt!

SIR MULBERRY *enters meeting* **EDDIE** *and* **PRINCESS CARABOO**.

SIR MULBERRY *(bowing before* **PRINCESS CARABOO**) Your Highness I took the liberty of procuring a set of engravings depicting the flora and fauna of your native lands.

He holds up the engravings for **PRINCESS CARABOO**'s *inspection. She is apparantly delighted.*

EDDIE Alas Her Highness cannot understand you, she has but few words of English.

SIR MULBERRY And yet she dimples most delightfully as she recognises the native creatures of her island home.

EDDIE Indeed she does, I'm sure Her Highness would thank you if she could, Mully.

LORD MARLBOROUGH. *An arrogant young aristocrat appraoches with an eccentric-looking scholar,* **MR IGEL**, *who is Dutch or can be played as German or Eastern European by changing references accordingly.*

LORD MARLBOROUGH Eddie! Mullbers! Perhaps I can be of some assistance!

EDDIE Lord Marlborough?

LORD MARLBOROUGH May I present to you Mr Igel of the Dutch East India Company, he don't look much, but they say the young pup's the world's foremost authority on dialects of the Egyptian and Caspian seas.

Sudden spotlight on **SIR CHARLES WORRALL**. *Everyone freezes.*

SIR CHARLES WORRALL *(referring to* **MR IGEL**) The ancient philosopher casts much scorn on what he calls the "professional liar", those who invent or allow falsehoods to flourish which bolster, unfairly, their professional reputations. "There are fewer more pitiful sights" he records in the Great Library of Alexandria "than that of the frightened fool puffing up his minimal talent with maximum wind".

Back to normality and **LORD MARLBOROUGH** *continues.*

LORD MARLBOROUGH There is not an accent, not a dialect, not a custom this Dutch chappie's not conversant in. *(To the crowd)* Eddie, or Mouse as we used to call him at school, has obliged us as far as an amateur is able but, ladies and gentlemen, I give you a colossus of the linguistic world. Thanks to my endeavours tonight the mystery is about to conclude. Here stands that man who will be able to translate for us this woman's remarkable history.

MR IGEL *talks to* **PRINCESS CARABOO** *in some strange but genuine dialect (gobbledygook the actor makes up) confident she will understand.*

There is no response from **PRINCESS CARABOO**.

He tries again.

No response from **PRINCESS CARABOO**.

And again.

Eventually **PRINCESS CARABOO** *lets forth a torrent of fake language.*

There's no response from **MR IGEL**. *He doesn't recognise her language (of course not. She's making it up on the spot but how's he to know this?) He feels his credibility is threatened. He's beginning to look uneasy.*

PRINCESS CARABOO *spouts even more nonsense.* **MR IGEL** *looks very uncomforatable at his inability to translate it.*

MR IGEL *(to* **EDDIE***. A lie)* It seems, sir, that you have been remarkably accurate in your assumptions. *(Heading for the door for a quick getaway)* I have little more to add.

LORD MARLBOROUGH *(icily dominating him)* Igel, I have brought you here at great expense, and you can contribute little more to the solving of this conundrum than *(Indicating* **EDDIE***)* our school runt!

MR IGEL *(aggresively florid)* Sir, you call into question my abilities? My reputation?

LORD MARLBOROUGH On the contrary we long to see a little of the linguistic expertise for which you are justly famed *(refering to* **EDDIE***)* rather than have you corroborate the lucky guesses of Mouse here.

MR IGEL *(winging it)* She speaks a Coptic Nubian dialect, nether written down or taught to outsiders. I have however managed to gain the trust of several native speakers and will endeavour to converse with her.

Song.

Caraboo

(to **PRINCESS CARABOO***)* Ikala wanos temi elashoo?

LORD MARLBOROUGH *(of* **MR IGEL***)*
KNEW, HE'D COME THROUGH.

EDDIE *(to* **MR IGEL***)* YOU ASK HER HIGHNESS'S NAME?

MR IGEL YES SIR, I DO.

IKALA WANOS TEMI ELASTROO?

EDDIE *(to* **PRINCESS CARABOO***)* REMEMBER? *(pointing to himself)* EDDIE – *(points to her and prompts)* PRINCESS –?

PRINCESS CARABOO *(in response)* CARABOO.

IKALAKE NOO-BA-LOO ARRAY.

EDDIE I THINK SHE'S PLEASED TO MEET YOU, SIR.

MR IGEL *(frosty)* SO I DEDUCED, MY FRIEND,

I'M SO GLAD THAT YOU CONCUR.

EDDIE COULD YOU ASK HER HIGHNESS IF SHE'D CARE TO DANCE?

LORD MARLBOROUGH EDDIE CAN'T YOU BUTT OUT NOW,

GIVE THE GROWN-UPS HERE A CHANCE?

A call and response dance number, with the other guests echoing the gobbledygook **MR IGEL** *and* **PRINCESS CARABOO** *spout.*

At the end **MR IGEL** *makes a hasty exit.*

Lights change.

Sometime later that same evening **LORD MARLBOROUGH** *and* **SIR MULBERRY** *corner* **EDDIE** *at the ball.* **PRINCESS CARABOO** *watches.*

Look at us, the three musketeers back together, again!

SIR MULBERRY I do believe the last time we gave you a dunking under the school pump, Mouse!

LORD MARLBOROUGH Happy days! So Mouse, is it true your father gambled away your inheritance?

EDDIE I have plans to reinstate the family business and the family honour.

LORD MARLBOROUGH Ah yes, your forthcoming exhibition. Do you really think there's an appetite for foreign vistas and tribal portraiture?

SIR MULBERRY Let's hope he don't make an exhibition of himself!

LORD MARLBOUROUGH Or that his pa's not spinning in his pauper's grave! No doubt your pretty dolly here will be the exhibition's main attraction. You want to watch it Mouse, or some young buck will have her off your hands.

They exit.

PRINCESS CARABOO *soothes* **EDDIE** *with a lullaby sung on an "ah" whilst stroking his forehead, he is entranced.*

Lullaby.

They kiss.

EDDIE Your kiss is like an angel's sigh.

PRINCESS CARABOO *(with a clear West Country accent)* Why thank you, my lover.

He bows to her – in that moment not realising the implication of what he's just heard.

She sails out of the room and is swamped by well wishers making any further interaction between them imposible.

Then the impact of her speaking hits him like a thunderbolt.

SIR CHARLES WORRALL *appears.*

SIR CHARLES WORRALL *(to the audience)* Ah! that sweet moment when a falsehood is revealed.

He goes.

"WAIT!"

EDDIE
WAIT! COME BACK
DID I... DID YOU?
I THOUGHT I HEARD,
NO, NO – GOD DAMN I DID!
IN THE MIDDLE OF A PERFECTLY
DELIGHTFUL NIGHT OF BLISS.
WHEN WE SHARED A KISS YOU TURN

AND BREAK MY HEART LIKE THIS!

I NEVER DREAMED THAT WORDS
AS INNOCUOUS AS THOSE.
COULD SO COMPLETELY BANISH HOPES
OF FUTURE NIGHTS' REPOSE.

I'M GIDDY AT THE THOUGHT OF IT
I DON'T THINK I'LL RECOVER.

FROM THE MOMENT THAT YOU TURNED TO ME
AND BLITHELY CALLED ME...

"LOVER"!

WHAT CAN IT MEAN?
WHY DID YOU SAY IT?
WHY DID YOU HOLD YOUR TONGUE BEFORE?
WHAT HAVE I DONE? HOW DO I PLAY IT?
LOOK AT ME I'M SHAKING, SWEATING,
SHORT OF BREATH AND QUAKING
MY KNEES ARE WEEK,
MY JAW IS ON THE FLOOR.

STOP! THIS MEANS!
I CAN'T... HAVE WE...?
HAS THIS ALL BEEN...?
I CANNOT BEAR THE THOUGHT.
MUST I CONCLUDE THAT THIS HAS BEEN
ONE TAWDRY CHEAP CHARADE?
MY FRIENDS, THIS TOWN, THERE'S MANY
HERE WILL TAKE THIS HARD.

A DARK DAY THIS
I WON'T FORGET
IT HURTS SO TO DISCOVER
YOU'VE HELPED TO PERPETRATE A MYTH
YOU MAY WELL SAY –

(spoken) "Thanks my lover"!

WELL, THAT'S ENOUGH.
YOU'VE HAD YOUR FUN NOW
TONIGHT YOUR CO-STAR LEAVES THE STAGE
ENJOY YOUR BOW, I THINK PERHAPS I

LACK THE KNACK REQUIRED TO PLAY THE FINAL PAGE.

Music doesn't resolve.

LADY ELIZABETH WORRALL *appears in a spotlight.*

LADY ELIZABETH WORRALL Dearest Edward, what has become of you? We have seen nothing of you at the Hall for weeks. All is progressing most satisfactorily here, although Her Highness still shows no aptitude for the English language. Only last night Sir Charles remarked that the only person to have made any progress with her was you. But despite her limited communication or perhaps because of it she continues to thrive. Lord Marlborough is most attentive. Teaching her to hunt – quite the warrior queen she turns out to be – and bedecking her in finery. I fear the poor man is rather smitten. Quite what the late Lord Marlborough would have had to say about it I dread to think. I do hope you give her a thought from time to time.

Vamp continues.

EDDIE From time to time...?!

Lights change. He is talking to **SIR MULBERRY**.

Mulberry, I hope I can convince you to extend the generous loan made to my late father. As you are well aware a series of unfortunate business decisions have entirely emptied my family's coffers.

SIR MULBERRY My dear Eddie. I have no wish to see you in the debtor's prison. Payments will be frozen for one month to allow you to find your feet but not a day longer.

EDDIE *(absent-mindedly quoting* **PRINCESS CARABOO** *in her West Country dialect)* "Thanks my lover".

SIR MULBERRY I beg your pardon?

EDDIE I... I mean. Thank you, sir. Diligently and timely payment of the outstanding sum will be...will be... *(distractedly quoting* **PRINCESS CARABOO** *again)* "my lover".

SIR MULBERRY What's that you say?!

EDDIE Sorry, sorry. "Will be my endeavour". Good day, and thank you.

SIR MULBERRY *exits.*

(sings. Chastising himself.) Oh get a grip!
HAS SHE BEWITCHED YOU?
THE JEZEBEL, THAT PAINED FRIGHT.
HOW DID I SLIP INTO THIS MUDDLE
WHERE EVERYTHING REMINDS ME
OF THE KIND OF LOOK SHE GAVE ME
WHEN SHE LEFT ME, GOOD AS DEAD,
THAT FATEFUL NIGHT.

His mind wanders again.

"Thank you, my lover"! "My lover"!?

He comes to his senses again with a start.

THIS CAN'T GO ON.
I MUST FORGET HER.
PRAY GOD, THAT MARLBOROUGH HASN'T GUESSED.
I MUST EXPOSE HER AND DISGRACE HER
BUT REALLY COULD I FACE HER?
FIGHT THE URGE TO JUST EMBRACE HER?
BEST STAY AWAY.
THE COWARD'S WAY
IS BEST.

Music resolves.

Lights change.

The **WORRALLS** *bustle in.*

We're at **EDDIE**'s *exhibition. No one has shown up.*

SIR CHARLES WORRALL Good day to you Edward, I hope we're not too late for the private view –

LADY ELIZABETH WORRALL It took an age before Lord Marlborough's carriage arrived for their expedition – *(she looks around)*

SIR CHARLES WORRALL I say…bit quiet isn't it?

LADY ELIZABETH WORRALL Edward? Where is everyone?

EDDIE Your Ladyship, the exhibition is a disaster. No one has accepted my invitation. And who can blame them? These past few weeks I have been a blithering idiot. Unable to concentrate, to communicate… My father would be ashamed.

LADY ELIZABETH WORRALL Edward dear, I do not wish to be indelicate but much as we loved him your father turned out to be an embezzler. Perhaps you have not developed his flair for persuasion yet but you, at least, do not deal in falsehoods.

EDDIE Forgive me I...

> **EDDIE** *looks queasy.*

SIR CHARLES WORRALL Are you alright Edward?

EDDIE I think. I think…this has all been a terrible mistake.

> *Suddenly* **LORD MARLBOROUGH** *bursts in with* **PRINCESS CARABOO** *on his arm surrounded by* **SIR MULBERRY, MR IGEL, LADY CATHERINE, LADY ELIZABETH WORRALL** *and* **LADY HARRIET**.

LORD MARLBOROUGH So then Mousey-me-lad, where's these blasted paintings you've been blathering on about?

EDDIE Lord Marlborough! Sir Mulberry! Mr Igel? Ladies! I didn't expect to see you here.

LORD MARLBOROUGH Well, I always say what's the point in doing the expected when there's dullards like you around to do that!

LADY ELIZABETH WORRALL What a lovely surprise, you seemed so set on taking her Highness to the races.

EDDIE *(icily to* **PRINCESS CARABOO***)* Good afternoon your Royal Highness, what an unexpected…honour.

LORD MARLBOROUGH Oh you're wasting your time Mouse, still can't get her to speak more then a few words of English and only then in that damnable foreign accent of hers. Don't she dress up nice though?

EDDIE Indeed. Exquisite. So…still a stranger to the English tongue?

SIR MULBERRY *(dirty joke)* Not a stranger to Marlborough's English tongue – know what I mean!

Cronies laugh.

EDDIE *can't stand the thought of this.*

EDDIE You'll have to forgive me, I'm afraid I'm not feeling well. If you could all please just go.

SIR MULBERRY Nonsense you little rodent.

LORD MARLBOROUGH Knock back a few glasses of champagne, that'll sort you. Lord and Lady W fancy a snifter? We've brought plenty. Sort 'em out Igel.

MR IGEL *gets everyone champagne.*

Besides the reason why I've given up an afternoon at the gee-gees is I've got a proposition for you, Mouse. I want to show Dolly off a bit, trouble is I can't have her stood there like a half-witted mute if some high society type wants to engage her in a little chit chat, can I? Igel's bally useless, the only one who's ever got any real sense out of her is you.

EDDIE So it would seem.

LORD MARLBOROUGH So what d'you say? Act as her interpreter on important occasions and in return… Well, I'll commission a portrait of Dolly here. Then if we unveil it at a fashionable party – you could have every filly in London battering down your doors for one of your daubings.

MR IGEL A most generous and brilliant scheme, your Lordship.

LORD MARLBOROUGH What do you say, Mouse? Translate for her when I'm showing her off and I'll ensure your masterpieces and my gal here are welcome in every drawing room in the land.

LADY ELIZABETH WORRALL *(excited)* Oh Edward!

SIR CHARLES WORRALL Very noble your Lordship, if I may say so.

LORD MARLBOROUGH *(to* **EDDIE***) If* you will be her voice.

LADY ELIZABETH WORRALL Oh, I know you can Edward, I know you can. Why one only has to see how attentive she is whenever you're speaking.

LORD MARLBOROUGH Do we have a deal? She can sit for the portrait this very afternoon.

EDDIE No!

LADY ELIZABETH WORRALL Edward?

EDDIE I can't. Don't you see, can't anyone see? She's… she's…

SIR CHARLES WORRALL She's what Edward?

LADY ELIZABETH WORRALL Don't you want to accept Lord Marlborough's generous offer?

EDDIE Wake up! All of you wake up! It's an act, it's all an act!

SIR CHARLES WORRALL Now, now his Lordship seems very genuine to me.

EDDIE This is…ridiculous. Can't you see what's in front of your eye? I mean… A PIRATE PRINCESS?!

LADY ELIZABETH WORRALL Oh I know, Edward. I know it's a lot to ask of you but I must confess I had been considering making you a similar proposal.

SIR CHARLES WORRALL Elizabeth?

LADY ELIZABETH WORRALL *(to* **EDDIE***)* I mean asking you to help the princess. Some summers ago the angels took my beautiful daughter from us.

SIR CHARLES WORRALL *(pained)* Elizabeth.

LADY ELIZABETH WORRALL Had she lived I would be presenting her at court this season. Well that was not to be but the good Lord sent me another child in this sweet, gentle creature. *(Indicating* **PRINCESS CARABOO***)* Now don't look at me like that Charles, I'm not a fool. I know that no one can replace…well anyway. I have no daughter to present and it has occurred to me that…it has occurred to me that perhaps if her Highness could master a little more English, if you could continue the progress you made Edward, I should very much like to help this young girl into society as I would have helped my own…my poor dear…

EDDIE I didn't translate anything. It was all… I was guessing.

LADY ELIZABETH WORRALL You are too modest Edward.

EDDIE No I…

LORD MARLBOROUGH Oh stop your confounded whining, you little runt. Be a man for once.

"YES"

SAY "YES".
COME ON SAY "YES".
PUT YOUR BEST FOOT FORWARD
GRAB SOME HAPPINESS.
DON'T BE A DOPE?
DON'T SIT AND MOPE
ITS TIME TO ACQUIESCE.
SAY "YES, YES, YES, YES, YES"!

DON'T SAY "NO"
THAT'S GOT TO GO.
LOOK THE WORLD STRAIGHT IN THE EYE AND SHOW
THAT ANYONE CAN LEAD THE BAND
AND BE A SUCCESS –

ALL

SAY "YES, YES, YES, YES, YES, YES"!

LORD MARLBOROUGH

NO "MAYBES"
DON'T BE A TEASE.
NO "UMM, I DON'T KNOW, I'M NOT SURE"
NOW, PLEASE,
YOU'VE GOT TO SQUARE UP TO YOUR FELLOW MAN
AND CLEARLY EXPRESS –

ALL

YES, YES, YES, YES, OH YES.

SIR CHARLES WORRALL Well, young Edward, will you act as her Highness's voice and capture her beauty in a portrait?

LORD MARLBOROUGH Do we have a deal, Sir Mouse?

SAY YES.
COME ON SAY YES.
DON'T STAND THERE LIKE
SOME DAMSEL IN DISTRESS.
HELP DOLLY AND WE'LL ALL ENDORSE
YOUR PAINTING PROWESS
SAY "YES, YES, YES, YES, YES"!

(to **PRINCESS CARABOO** *)* Wonder what you'd have to say, Dolly?

Promoting her.

JUST SAY "YES"
COME ON SAY –

PRINCESS CARABOO   *(tentatively as if the word is foreign to her)*
YES.

LORD MARLBOROUGH
SEE DOLLY HERE'S BEEN MAKING SOME PROGRESS.
DON'T BE SUCH A NINNY, MOUSE
ANTICIPATE SUCCESS.
JUST SAY –

He points at **PRINCESS CARABOO** *to cue her.*

PRINCESS CARABOO
YES, YES, YES, YES, YES, YES, YES.

Vamp continues.

LADY ELIZABETH WORRALL   Why don't we give Edward a chance to talk to her Highness alone, assess how her language skills are improving?

LORD MARLBOROUGH   Can't hurt, right everyone clear out, let the dog sniff the rabbit. *(Lightly to* **EDDIE** *who he does not regard as a threat)* Obviously lay one finger on her and I'll feed your squidgy bits to my wolf hounds. With you attached.

LADY ELIZABETH WORRALL   Oh Edward, I do hope you can find it in your heart to help her Highness.

All but **EDDIE** *and* **PRINCESS CARABOO** *exit.*

SIR CHARLES WORRALL *in his spotlight.*

SIR CHARLES WORRALL   For Aracticus every lie has its Nikandros moment, a tipping point where the deception will either disintegrate, disarmed by the actions of a benign outside influence, or else it will survive the threat to grow stronger, extending the range and depth of its impact.

He is gone.

EDDIE *and* **PRINCESS CARABOO** *are alone.*

EDDIE I don't know what to say to you.

PRINCESS CARABOO *(West Country accent in private)* Seems to me like you said plenty. I wouldn't be in this mess if you hadn't gone so doe-eyed when you got a sight of me. I could have slipped away when the coast was clear but you had to start your showing off 'bout all your learning from your travels. Getting the old 'uns all excited.

EDDIE You could have intervened. Told the truth.

PRINCESS CARABOO Oh and what? Be whipped from here to Taunton for vagrancy? Or worse…

LADY ELIZABETH WORRALL *and the girls pass through, tipsy on champagne.*

She sings.

THE WRETCHED FRENCH
WE ALL AGREE
ARE LOATHED TO SAY IT
HENCE OUR VICTORY.
FORGIVE ME IF I FAIL TO QUITE
PRONOUNCE IT PROPERLY
SAY "OUI –

ALL

OUI, OUI, OUI, MAIS OUI"!

Oops sorry, we're interrupting.

She ushers all but **PRINCESS CARABOO** *and* **EDDIE** *off.*

PRINCESS CARABOO You've no idea what it's like for a young woman, penniless, no one to turn to. People like you taking advantage.

EDDIE In what way do you imagine I have been advantaged?

PRINCESS CARABOO You wanted me, admit it. You saw me and you wanted me. What's the matter, am I not putting it pretty enough? At least that lord – at least he's honest 'bout what he wants.

> **LORD MARLBOROUGH** *crosses the stage with the men. All merry with drink.*

LORD MARLBOROUGH THE GERMANS? AH!

> YOU'LL BE A STAR

> IF YOU CAN GREET EACH MORNING WITH A JA.

MR IGEL

> AND JUST FORGET
> THAT RUSSIAN "NET"
> WHEN TALKING TO A TSAR –

MEN

> SAY DA, DA, DA, DA, DA!

> *The revellers exit.*

EDDIE You are an entirely reprehensible young woman.

PRINCESS CARABOO And you're a pompous, puffed up little weasel. Imagine letting them throw me a party. Once they'd got that idea in their heads no one left me alone, dressing me, bathing me, servants looking in on me like I was a travelling circus.

EDDIE I will not take responsibility for this charade.

PRINCESS CARABOO No? Well you should. What about you egging on that language fella. Don't know how I pulled that off in front of everyone.

EDDIE Well, you're obviously very adept at telling lies.

PRINCESS CARABOO Seems like I am. And you're going to help me tell a few more.

EDDIE I most certainly am not.

The others swing through again.

SIR CHARLES WORRALL
IN HINDUSTAN THEY ALL SAY GEE
TO EACH EXPRESS A POSITIVITY.

LADY CATHERINE
ITALIANS SAY THE SAME AS SPAIN
COINCIDENTALLY

ALL
SAY SI, SI ,SI. SI ,SI, SI.

LADY ELIZABETH WORRALL *(spoken)* Well Edward, your answer.

Sung.
PLEASE DON'T KEEP US IN SUSPENSE
BY FORCING US TO GUESS.

ALL
SAY "YES, YES, YES, YES,
SAY YES".

EDDIE A little longer, please. I am just assessing the princess's thinking.

The two are left alone again.

PRINCESS CARABOO Think I'm walking away now, after all I've been through? I'm milking this for every penny I can get.

EDDIE Why did you kiss me? Sing to me like that?

PRINCESS CARABOO I... I don't know, don't start twisting things again. You're going to help me out of this mess. It's the least you can do.

EDDIE You think I can save you?

PRINCESS CARABOO I don't need saving. Haven't I proved that? From now on I'm taking control.

"MY OWN PERSON"

She sings.

NO MORE BEING SHOUTED AT
AND TOLD WHAT I SHOULD DO.
A PUPPET FOR WHO'D EVER PULL THE STRINGS.
TIME TO LEAVE THE SHADOWS.

I AM NO-ONE'S FOOL NO MORE
I'M READY NOW TO FACE SO MANY THINGS.

I AM MY OWN PERSON
NOBODY SPEAKS FOR ME.
THE ONE WHO'S TAKING CHARGE OF THINGS IS ME NOW.
I HAVE MY OWN OPINIONS
AND MY THOUGHTS BELONG TO ME
DON'T NEED NO-ONE TO SHAPE MY DESTINY NOW.

AND EVERYONE WHO'D DRAG ME DOWN
AND TELL ME TAKE IT SLOW.
THEY'LL FIND OUT SOON THAT THEY DON'T REALLY KNOW
  ME.
I'VE HAD ENOUGH OF HOLDING BACK
NOT TREADING ON THEIR TOES
I DON'T NEED THEM OR ANYONE TO SHOW ME
WHO I SHOULD BE.

I AM MY OWN PERSON
LOOKING OUT FOR NUMBER ONE.
BUT EDDIE, WON'T YOU JOIN ME ON THE RIDE NOW?
I PROMISE YOU ADVENTURE,
AND WHEN THE GOING'S TOUGH,
I'LL KEEP YOU SAFE BUT YOU HAVE TO DECIDE NOW.

I KNOW I'M ALWAYS TROUBLE
WOULD YOU HAVE ME LIKE THE REST?
COWERING IN MY CORNER SQUEAKING "YES, SIR"
I WANT TO BE THE MISCHIEF MAKER,
LET THE WORLD COMPLAIN

"WHO'S THE ONE WHO'S SHOUTING? IS IT JUST HER?
OUT IN THE RAIN AGAIN".

FEMALE BACKING VOICES

I AM MY OWN PERSON
NOBODY SPEAKS FOR ME
DON'T NEED ANOTHER STANDING IN MY STEAD NOW.
I HAVE MY OWN FEELINGS
AND MY LIFE BELONGS TO ME.
DON'T NEED PERMISSION, I CAN FORGE AHEAD NOW!

PRINCESS CARABOO

TAKE A CHANCE
LEAD THE DANCE
COME ON AND JOIN ME
BANG THE DRUM
STAND TALL AND PROUD AND SAY –

I AM MY OWN PERSON
NOBODY SPEAKS FOR ME
DON'T NEED ANOTHER STANDING IN MY STEAD NOW.
I HAVE MY OWN FEELINGS
AND MY LIFE BELONGS TO ME.
DON'T NEED PERMISSION, I CAN FORGE AHEAD NOW!

CAN'T YOU LEAVE THE PAST BEHIND
AND FOLLOW ME.

End of Act One

ACT TWO
Scene 1

The company sing –

"TRUTH"

ALL

THE TRUTH IS STRANGER THAN FICTION
YOU COULDN'T MAKE THIS UP.
YOU'VE GOT TO BE CAREFUL
DRINKING FROM THE LIAR'S CUP.
IF IT'S EASY TO SWALLOW
BEWARE OF THE STING.
A ROGUE CAN MAKE YOU, WITH A SMILE,
BELIEVE IN ANYTHING.

HATTY

SO WHO IS WHAT?
AND WHAT IS WHO?

ALL

AND WHO'S BEEN TELLING LIES
TO YOU?

SIR CHARLES WORRALL

IF WE CAN'T TRUST THE ONES WE LOVE
THEN WHAT IS LOVE ABOUT?
THE COWARD'S WAY IS TRUST NO-ONE
AND TRY TO CATCH THEM OUT.
BUT THE BRAVER GIVES THE STRANGER
THE BENEFIT OF DOUBT.
NOT EVERYONE'S DECEITFUL
THEY CAN LOOK YOU IN THE EYE.

ALL

MOST PEOPLE WANT THE BEST FOR YOU –
WAIT! WE TELL A LIE.

THE TRUTH IS STRANGER THEN FICTION
YOU COULDN'T MAKE THIS UP.
YOU'VE GOT TO BE CAREFUL
DRINKING FROM THE LIAR'S CUP.

MR IGEL

IF IT'S EASY TO SWALLOW
BEWARE OF THE STING.

OSVALDO AGATHIAS

A ROGUE CAN MAKE YOU, WITH A SMILE,
BELIEVE IN ANYTHING.

ALL

SO WHO IS WHAT?
AND WHAT IS WHO?
AND WHO'S BEEN TELLING LIES
TO YOU?

SIR CHARLES WORRALL

WELL, ARE YOU ALWAYS HONEST, PRAY
IN ALL YOU SAY AND DO?

LORD MARLBOROUGH

WHEN WE NEED TO WIN THE DAY WE
LIE TO GET US THROUGH.

LADY ELIZABETH WORRALL

IS THE FACE YOU SHOW THE WORLD
THE REAL FACE OF YOU?

PRINCESS CARABOO AND **EDDIE**

YOU SHOULDN'T JUDGE A LIAR,
IT COULD BE YOU WHO'LL FIND
THE TRUTH'S A LITTLE TRICKIER
WHEN YOUR LIES UNWIND.

ALL

> THE TRUTH IS STRANGER THEN FICTION
> YOU COULDN'T MAKE THIS UP
> YOU'D BETTER BE CAREFUL
> DRINKING FROM THE LIAR'S CUP.
> IF IT'S EASY TO SWALLOW
> BEWARE OF THE STING
> A ROGUE CAN MAKE YOU, WITH A SMILE,
> BELIEVE IN ANYTHING.
> SO WHO IS WHAT
> AND WHAT IS WHO
> AND WHO WILL YOU BE LYING TO?

SIR CHARLES WORRALL *in a spotlight.*

SIR CHARLES WORRALL "How little it takes," writes Aracticus in the third century BC "to perpetrate a myth. Why, sometimes, one need only lend a slight nod, a gentle smile or even, merely one's presence to aid the transition from local myth to universal legend."

He goes.

Scene 2

EDDIE*'s business premises. Succesful now.*

LORD MARLBOROUGH *bursts in on him.*

LORD MARLBOROUGH So Mouse. The portrait!

EDDIE I wish I could help you, Marlborough I really do. But I'm afraid I can have nothing to do with your... little project. On moral grounds.

LORD MARLBOROUGH On what?

EDDIE Moral grounds. Morals. The little checks and balances that ensure we treat our fellow man with decency and respect.

I don't expect you to understand, let's hope that one day the princess masters enough English to make things clear. I'm sure whatever scruples she picked up on the mysterious island of Caraboo or wherever it is she comes from will inform her conduct at some point.

LORD MARLBOROUGH *(not listening)* Ain't she got great boobies though? *(Beat)* Sorry Mouse what were you saying? Attention wandered a bit there. You'll start Dolly's portrait today? Perfecto! I'm off to the gee-gees, can pick her up around five.

EDDIE Will you please listen to me. I really cannot, will not –

LORD MARLBOROUGH Splendid that's all settled then. A word if I may. This island of Dolly's... *(confidently)* Caravan?

EDDIE Caraboo.

LORD MARLBOROUGH That's the chappie! Where do they stand on the old pre-marital relations?

EDDIE I beg your pardon?

LORD MARLBOROUGH You know, the old "congress before wedlock" business? Every time I lay a finger on her she scratches and spits like a Cardiff whore!

EDDIE I'm glad to hear she knows some restraint. One might almost imagine she'd grab anything that might advantage her.

LORD MARLBOROUGH *(still not listening)* Trouble is she then flashes me that smile and the look in her eyes is pure "ride-a-cock-horse." Know what I mean? Don't know where I stand.

EDDIE I'm sure we'll find the Caroobian custom is to make a declaration of one's wealth before engaging with the princess, perhaps a diamond bracelet or a priceless rare orchid might prove your worth.

LORD MARLBOROUGH Think so? What's an orchid?

EDDIE Very, very expensive.

LORD MARLBOROUGH Splendid. I'll get some in. See you at five. Tell her I'll be back with a –

EDDIE An orchid!

LORD MARLBOROUGH Don't let me catch you staring at her backside!

Thinking of **PRINCESS CARABOO**.

Ain't she though?

EDDIE *sets up his painter's easel and debates with himself.*

"PAINTED LADY"

A PORTRAIT OF THE PRINCESS CARABOO!
HOW DO I PAINT WHAT ISN'T THERE?
HOW CAN I LEARN TO SEE
A MASK THE OTHERS SEE
WHEN I ALONE CAN SEE THE TEAR.

Pronounced "tear" as in ripped.

WHAT IS HER GAME, THIS PRINCESS CARABOO?
A RAGGED PACK OF TANGLED LIES
WHY SHOULD I JOIN THE DANCE
GIVE HER A FIGHTING CHANCE
AND MASTER HER DISGUISE?

PRINCESS CARABOO *enters with* **BETTY** *and* **HATTY** *who arrange her for the portrait during the next verse.* **EDDIE** *watches, exasperated and sings to himself unheard by the others.*

HOW DO YOU DRAW SOMEONE WHO ISN'T THERE
WHY SHOULD I HELP THE STORY FLY?
PERPETUATE A LIE,
CREATE AN ALIBI,
WHEN ONLY I CAN RAISE THE CRY.
WELL, I WON'T DO IT PRINCESS CARABOO
PAINT YOUR DECEITFUL FLASHING EYES
I'M NOT A CHARLATAN
OR YOUR AUTOMATON
NO, NO I WILL NOT PAINT YOUR LIES.

PRINCESS CARABOO You think you're so superior, don't you? When I saw you I thought, he's different, he's got a kind face. You're the biggest snob of the lot.

EDDIE *(icy)* Perhaps, if you can momentarily focus on someone other then yourself, you'll see that I have recently discovered the father I idolised was in a fact defrauding his business associates. I do not intend to follow his lead.

PRINCESS CARABOO Perhaps he had his reasons.

EDDIE A fear of poverty, a loss of dignity. Storms I will weather if bad fortune befalls me. Our family have endured it before.

PRINCESS CARABOO *(contemptuously)* "Bad fortune"? –

"UNDERSTANDING"

YOU REALLY HAVE NO IDEA DO YOU?
RICH LITTLE BOY,

DOWN TO YOUR LAST SILVER SPOON WERE YOU?
YOUR LAST PRETTY TOY?
THAT'S NOT POVERTY,
WHAT IT'S LIKE TO NEED.
THINK YOU HAD IT BAD DO YOU?
THIS LIFE YOU LEAD
IT'S NOTHING
TRY LIFE ON THE STREET
WITH A BABE THAT YOU CAN'T FEED.

EDDIE *(spoken)* A baby. But… who was the… couldn't the father…?

PRINCESS CARABOO *(spoken)* There was no bleedin' orchids I can tell you. I was just a maid, his property till he threw me aside. A man just like his Lordship.

THE SAME LOOK IN HIS EYE
THE SAME TILT OF THE HEAD
THE SAME ICE IN HIS HEART
ALL SENSITIVITY DEAD.
HE THREW ME ASIDE THOUGH I CARRIED HIS CHILD
NOT EVEN A BACKWARD GLANCE.
WHEN I GET A CHANCE TO CRUSH PEOPLE LIKE THAT
BY GOD, I GRAB THE CHANCE.

BACK THEN I WAS A GIRL
HE MADE ME FEEL LIKE A WIFE
SO WHEN HE THREW ME AWAY
THE HURT CUT ME DEEP LIKE A KNIFE.
AND SO MANY GIRLS IN MY PLIGHT
NEVER PULL THROUGH BUT YOU SEE
I HAD MY BABY. MY DEAR LITTLE GIRL.
TILL THAT PLACE TOOK HER FROM ME.

EDDIE What place?

PRINCESS CARABOO *(spoken)* You don't know you're born. Come with me.

EDDIE *(spoken)* Where are we going?

PRINCESS CARABOO *(spoken)* The *(with disdain)* "Municipal
Housing for the Poor".

EDDIE *(spoken)* The workhouse? What's that to you?

PRINCESS CARABOO It's the only choice for girls like me.
Come on.

She leads him off.

HATTY, MRS CATESBY *and* **BETTY** *enter.*

BETTY *(sings)*
AND HER EYES FLASHED
AND SHE LED HIM TO SUCH SCENES OF DESPAIR.

MRS CATESBY
A MONOLITHIC EDIFICE OF COLD, GREY STONE
A PUTRID STENCH FILLED THE AIR.
HERE WAS WHERE WE HOUSED THE POOR,
OUR FELLOW MAN, OUR BROTHERS.

HATTY
FORCING WIVES FROM HUSBANDS,
CHILDREN FROM THEIR MOTHERS.

BETTY
AND HE WEPT BECAUSE –
HE HAD NO IDEA!

We see **PRINCESS CARABOO** *and* **EDDIE** *as if looking
around the workhouse, as the three women sing -*

ALL THREE
NO IDEA

HATTY
THAT HUMAN LIFE WAS HELD SO CHEAP.

ALL THREE
NO IDEA.

BETTY
HOW THEY MUST TOIL TO EARN THEIR KEEP.

ALL THREE

NO IDEA.

MRS CATESBY

THE UNIFORMS, A SHAME LIKE BRANDING
SHE WAS RIGHT, IN WHAT SHE SAID.

HATTY

HE HAD NO UNDERSTANDING.

EDDIE

I HAD NO IDEA.

As **PRINCESS CARABOO** *describes events they're shown in dumbshow with* **BETTY** *representing* **PRINCESS CARABOO**, *a bundle representing the baby,* **MRS CATESBY** *and* **HATTY** *as the workhouse attendants pulling it from her and* **RICHARD** *entering as the chaplain who takes away the "baby".*

PRINCESS CARABOO

THERE'S NO COMPASSION HERE
THERE'S NOTHING WARM
THERE IS NO PITY
IN THEIR LOOK OF SCORN.
UNTIL MY DEATH BED I'LL ALWAYS SEE
THE MOMENT THEY PULLED HER FROM ME.
I BEG THEM NOT TO, THE BABE WAS SICK
BUT REGULATIONS ARE VERY STRICT
I TRIED TO STEAL HER A BIT OF GRUEL
TO KEEP HER STRENGTH UP
I WAS A FOOL.
NO HAPPY ENDINGS FOR SUCH AS ME,
I MUST BE PUNISHED,
I'D SINNED, YOU SEE
THEY TOOK HER FROM ME, THE LITTLE WAIF
THE CHAPLIN PROMISED THEY'D KEEP HER SAFE
I KNEW THEY WOULDN'T
SHE NEVER CRIED
AT DAWN THE NEXT DAY
I HEARD SHE'D -

ALL *but* **PRINCESS CARABOO** *and* **EDDIE** *exit.*

(spoken) I ran out into the cold October rain with nothing. I begged, maybe I stole a little, told a few lies on my travels but I never meant no one harm. And I was no trouble to nobody till now. *(Beat)* I don't know why I'm in this mess but I am, whether it's God's fault or yours or that Spaniard…but I've got to make the best of it. I can't go back, Eddie. I got to grab this chance for a better life. Say you'll help me, Eddie. Eddie with the kind eyes. You won't turn me in will you?

EDDIE I… I… No. I won't.

PRINCESS CARABOO I need you, someone I can trust. I can trust you, can't I?

EDDIE Are you going to break my heart?

PRINCESS CARABOO You're not so stupid you'd fall for me are you? Oh, look at the mopey look on your face. *(Strong)* Pull yourself together. Can I trust you or what?

EDDIE Yes.

PRINCESS CARABOO *(happy)* I knew it. When I saw them bullying you. That night at the Worrall's party. I had to kiss you.

They kiss.

EDDIE It gets me all muddled when you do that.

SIR CHARLES WORRALL *in a spotlight.*

SIR CHARLES WORRALL There is a perception, Aracticus councils, that the thriving lie brings happiness and contentment to the successful liar. This, he points out, is seldom true. In a universe built on the quicksand of false attainment and expectation peace of mind is seldom possible.

He exits.

Sound and lights take us to London.

A dingy tavern. The Spaniard staggers in holding his head.

A serving girl, **MEG**, *accosts him.*

MEG   *(chattering in a London accent)* Oh you're up, are you then, Señor? About time, it's past noon. Innkeeper sent me to tell you your rent's due on this room Saturday and you're three weeks behind.

OSVALDO AGATHIAS *groans.*

(beat) Sore head? Not surprised the amount of ale you put away last night. *(Sweeping)* By the way I saw your lady friend earlier, the one you're always going on about, stepping into a carriage on The Strand everyone calling out her name. Oooh so elegant she looked. You'd think she'd be a bit of a country bumpkin but no, all done up beautiful for London society –

"WHEN"

OSVALDO AGATHIAS   *(chasing the girl out)*
THAT'S IT, GET OUT, ENOUGH!

Alone.

DON'T WANT TO HEAR ABOUT
THE DRESS SHE WORE
WHAT BALL YOU SAW HER GOING TO.
DON'T WANT TO HEAR ABOUT THE LITTLE WAVES,
(THE) COURTLY KNAVES
SHE'S TALKING TO.
I'VE HAD IT UP TO HERE WITH HEARING OF
THE TRIUMPH OF HER GREAT SUCCESS
JUST WANT TO FIGURE OUT THE PERFECT TIME
TO POUNCE AND CAUSE THE MOST DISTRESS.

An imaginary **PRINCESS CARABOO** *enters to tango with him.*

FOR THERE WAS A TIME THE PRINCESS WAS NOT WHAT YOU
    SAW
WHEN SHE CLUNG TO ME
TO SAVE HER FROM THE LAW
WE WERE TWO BEGGARS THROWN IN A COUNTY JAIL
HER FLASHING EYES GAVE ME A PLAN DOWN TO THE LAST
    DETAIL.

WE'D GET PEOPLE THINKING THAT SHE WAS A PRINCESS OF
    OLD
THE ENGLISH ARE STUPID IT WASN'T SO HARD, WE WERE
    BOLD
I WEAVE A STORY OF PIRATES, THE SHIPWRECK THAT
    BROUGHT HER THERE
THEN WHEN THE FOOLS TURNED THEIR BACKS WE'D SNEAK
    OFF WITH THE SILVERWARE.

HOW WAS I TO KNOW
SHE'D GO TOO FAR
BECOME THIS STAR,
THE LATEST CRAZE.

SHE WAS SUPPOSED TO LEAVE HER BED THAT NIGHT
IN DEAD OF NIGHT WE'D RANSACK THE PLACE.
INSTEAD SHE THINKS NO, NO
I'LL PLAY THIS LONG
AND PLAY IT COOL
LET OUT THE ROPE
FORGET THE SPANISH PEASANT, SO HE LOVES ME
WELL? SO WHAT?
I'LL FIND ANOTHER DOPE.

NOW I MUST LIVE LIKE A RAT IN THE MISERABLE PLIGHT
WHILE SHE SQUANDERS THE LOOT FROM OUR LIES THAT IS
    HALF MINE BY RIGHTS.

WELL YOU HAD BETTER
TAKE A LOT OF CARE
DEAR PRINCESS FAIR
I'M CHECKING ALL.
I'M WAITING TILL THE MOMENT'S HERE
TO REAPPEAR FOR WRECKING ALL.

SO SIP YOUR FANCY WINE
AND TAKE YOUR TIME
ENJOY YOURSELF
MY LITTLE FRIEND.
IT ISN'T A QUESTION OF WILL I

Imaginary **PRINCESS CARABOO** *exits.*

DESTROY YOU
BUT MORE OF WHEN.

IT ISN'T A QUESTION OF WILL I
DESTROY YOU
BUT MORE OF WHEN.

SIR CHARLES WORRALL *in a spotlight.*

SIR CHARLES WORRALL   If one must deal in lies, and Aracticus concedes this may, alas, be man's natural state, there must be a moment of triumph, of "getting away with it" in the popular parlance. "Dare we enjoy it to the full?" The ancient muses. "Or are we always doomed to be haunted by fear of discovery"

He exits.

An anteroom of a very grand London ball.

In the scene change.

FLUNKY My lords, ladies and gentlemen, dinner is served.

EDDIE *and* **PRINCESS CARABOO** *triumphant, rush in to grab a few moments in private, to enjoy their success and to gloat!*

"FABULOUS"

EDDIE
DID YOU SEE HER?

PRINCESS CARABOO
> HOW HE –

EDDIE
> DID SHE REALLY?

BOTH
> FABULOUS!
> OH, THIS PARTY THAT WE CALL A LIFE!

EDDIE
> WHO COULD HAVE DREAMED EV'RY NIGHT
> WOULD BE SUCH AN ADVENTURE
> OUR EVERY VENTURE WINS A PRIZE.

PRINCESS CARABOO
> I'M HELD IN A SPELL AND I FELL
> WE'RE THE CHAMPAGNE AVENGERS,
> EVERY TRIUMPH A SURPRISE.

EDDIE
> I RULE THE WORLD WITH YOU
> WE ARE LIKE GODS.

PRINCESS CARABOO
> THE SLIGHTEST WORD FROM YOU
> AND HEAVEN NODS
> APPROVAL.
> WHO COULD HAVE DREAMED EVERY NIGHT
> COULD BE SUCH AN OCCASION?
> SUCH OVATIONS –

BOTH
> – SUCH DELIGHT

EDDIE
> AND WHY IS THIS HAPPENING?
> HOW IS THIS HAPPENING?
> TAKING SUCCESS IN MY STRIDE?
> WELL, I HAVE TO CONCEDE

PRINCESS CARABOO
> I'VE BEGUN TO BELIEVE

EDDIE
IT'S 'CAUSE YOU NEVER LEAVE MY SIDE.

They snap back into role as **LORD MARLBOROUGH**
arrives with William Pitt the Younger.

LORD MARLBOROUGH Ah, there she is, there's Dolly.
Mouse, where have you been hiding her? *(to* **PITT***)*
Here she is, Bill. Gal, I was telling you about.

PITT Enchanting

LORD MARLBOROUGH Ain't she?

EDDIE *(to* **PRINCESS CARABOO***)* Your Highness, this brilliant
young man is Mr William Pit, the Younger. *(As if trying
to make her understand)* Politics, politicians. Mr Pitt is a
fine example of a *(fake language)* Nicle-ackle-poot-plop.

PRINCESS CARABOO Awww. *(Pointing to* **PITT***)* Nicle-ackle-
poot-plop?

EDDIE *and* **PRINCESS CARABOO** *trying not to laugh.*

EDDIE Oh most definitely. One of the biggest nicle-ackle-
poot-plops around.

PRINCESS CARABOO *(smiles sweetly at* **PITT** *and adresseses him
in pidgeon English)* You politician, mighty leader. Where
you lead Caraboo will follow.

PITT *(besotted)* My goodness, me. Your Highness…
(to **MARLBOROUGH***)* she's…well quite, quite charming.
Where did you say she was from?

EDDIE The Island of Caraboo, Mr Pitt.

LORD MARLBOROUGH This is Eddie "The Mouse". He's
travelled a bit in Dolly's part of the world so I bring
him along to translate.

PITT I'm so glad you did. *(Of* **PRINCESS CARABOO***)* And
as for this creature… Marlborough won't you bring
her for dinner on Sunday? It's about time we found

you a seat in Parliament. And I'm sure we can find something amongst the treasures of the Foreign Office to delight her Highness.

EDDIE Her Majesty particularly enjoys emeralds.

PITT Does she indeed, we must see what we can do. (*As he wanders off*) Think about it Marlborough, a parliamentary seat.

THE WORRALLS *appear.*

LADY ELIZABETH WORRALL Edward, won't you bring the princess to meet Lady Cavendish, I know she'll be enchanted.

SIR CHARLES WORRALL Elizabeth, shouldn't you rest a while? You know the doctor said not to exert yourself.

LADY ELIZABETH WORRALL Nonsense I'm as right as rain now. Your Highness, would you do us the honour?

LORD MARLBOROUGH Parade her round a bit then, Mouse.

LADY ELIZABETH WORRALL (*As she exits with* **SIR CHARLES WORRALL**, **EDDIE** *and* **PRINCESS CARABOO**) Lady Cavendish has some very beautiful racehorses, your Highness. You'll enjoy them very much.

LORD MARLBOROUGH *alone.*

LORD MARLBOROUGH (*sings*)
WHO COULD HAVE DREAMED EV'RY NIGHT
WOULD BE SUCH AN ADVENTURE.
HOW EACH GENT'D CATCH HER EYE.
I'M HELD IN A SPELL AND I'VE FELL
I'M THE TOAST OF THE EMPIRE
STILL I S'POSE IT'S NO SURPRISE.
SHE'LL RULE THE WORLD WITH ME
AINT THIS A FARCE?
HOW I'M ENRAPTURED BY
HER BEAUTIFUL ARSE,
COMPLETELY.

WHO COULD HAVE DREAMED EVERY NIGHT
COULD BE SUCH AN OCCASION
SUCH OVATIONS, SUCH DELIGHT.
AND WHY IS THIS HAPPENING?
HOW IS THIS HAPPENING?
I'M WINED AND DINED FAR AND WIDE.
WELL, I HAVE TO CONCEDE
I'VE BEGUN TO BELIEVE
IT'S 'CAUSE SHE NEVER LEAVES MY SIDE.

He exits.

As **THE WORRALLS** *enter.*

LADY ELIZABETH WORRALL My dear, did you see how her Ladyship was charmed?

SIR CHARLES WORRALL She's a credit to you Elizabeth.

LADY ELIZABETH WORRALL Do you think she retained any of the etiquette I tried to teach her? I never know if she comprehends me but –

SIR CHARLES WORRALL My dear, she has remembered everything you taught her. She's a very superior type of a girl. She is royalty after all.

LADY ELIZABETH WORRALL Yes, yes I must remember that but, Oh Charles I can't help thinking of her as our – Charlotte would have been her age if –

SIR CHARLES WORRALL My love. You will fatigue yourself again and you know what the doctor said. Let us concentrate on what is before us not what might have been.

BOTH

WHO COULD HAVE DREAMED EV'RY NIGHT
WOULD BE SUCH AN ADVENTURE.
HER EVERY VENTURE JUST DELIGHTS.
THEY'RE HELD IN HER SPELL,
WHO COULD TELL
OUR SUCCESSFUL INDENTURE

WOULD SCALE SUCH GIDDY HEIGHTS?

Adoringly to each other.

I'D GIVE THE WORLD FOR YOU,
MY TURTLE DOVE.
THE SLIGHTEST WORD FROM YOU
FILLS ME WITH LOVE
AS ALWAYS.

WHO COULD HAVE DREAMED
ON THAT NIGHT WHEN SHE DIED
WE WOULD EVER
LEARN TO EVER SMILE AGAIN?
AND WHY IS THIS HAPPENING?
HOW IS THIS HAPPENING?
WHY AM I BURSTING WITH PRIDE?
WELL I HAVE TO CONCEDE
I'VE BEGUN TO BELIEVE
IT'S CAUSE SHE NEVER LEAVES OUR SIDE.

THE WORRALLS *exit.*

EDDIE *and* **PRINCESS CARABOO** *run on, giggling in private about their conquests –*

PRINCESS CARABOO

OH MY GOD, NO! –

EDDIE

DID HE ASK YOU OUTSIDE?

PRINCESS CARABOO

WHEN SHE TOLD YOU THAT –

EDDIE

I THOUGHT I'D DIED

The company enter from the ballroom all besotted with **PRINCESS CARABOO**.

ALL

WHO COULD HAVE DREAMED THAT ONE GIRL
COULD ENLIVEN OUR LIVES SO.

SHE ARRIVES AND OH THE STIR!
SUDDENLY SOMEHOW THE AIR
IS ALIVE WITH ROMANCE AND
IT IS ALL DUE TO HER.
MIRACLES BROUGHT HER HERE
WISHES CAME TRUE
GIVING US HOPE AGAIN
WE CAN PURSUE
OUR DREAMS TOO.

Couples turn to each other including **LORD MARLBOROUGH** *with* **PRINCESS CARABOO**.

EVER SINCE I LEARNT THAT LIFE
IS INDEED AN ADVENTURE.
I KEEP THINKING OF YOU
AND WHY IS THIS HAPPENING?
HOW IS THIS HAPPENING?
WHEN YOU ARE BY MY SIDE?
WELL I HAVE TO CONCEDE
I'VE BEGUN TO BELIEVE –

LORD MARLBOROUGH

THAT YOU OUGHT TO BE MY BRIDE.

Music does not resolve.

EDDIE Marlborough?

LORD MARLBOROUGH Yes, why not. Mouse, translation please. Tell her, ask her, if she…ask her if she'll marry me.

EDDIE Are you sure? I mean…

LORD MARLBOROUGH Quite sure, Mouse, thank you.

EDDIE But I mean… What if she loves another?

LORD MARLBOROUGH Who? What are you blithering on about? Don't be tiresome, just remember who got you in here. Ask her to marry me, damn you.

EDDIE *looks* **PRINCESS CARABOO** *in the eye.*

EDDIE His Lordship says… His Lordship asks if you would do him the honour of…shad ak os de remano dilati – ai?

They stare at each other. Tension between them.

(repeating the gobbledygook) Shad ak os de remano dilati – ai?

Again they stare at each other. Tension between them.

LORD MARLBOROUGH What the devil's the hold up? Ask her again.

EDDIE Shad ak os de remano dilati – ai?

Silence.

(asking her to choose between yes or no) Bryki or zoolaki?

They stare at each other. He repeats.

Bryki or zoolaki?

PRINCESS CARABOO Zoolaki.

EDDIE Zoolaki?

PRINCESS CARABOO *(pause. Making up her mind)* Zoolaki.

Silence. They look at each other.

LORD MARLBOROUGH Well, she choose me? What did she say?

EDDIE *(truthfully)* I… I don't know.

LORD MARLBOROUGH What the blazes do you mean, you don't –

But **PRINCESS CARABOO** *crosses to him, kneels in front of him, smiles up at him and says –*

PRINCESS CARABOO Zoolaki.

LORD MARLBOROUGH   *(beaming. Understanding he's been accepted)* Ah zoolaki.

THE DELIGHTED CROWD   Zoolaki!

They applaud.

LORD MARLBOROUGH   Tell her she's a very lucky girl.

Everyone but **EDDIE** *laughs.*

EDDIE   *(covering his heartbreak)* If you'll excuse me, your Lordship, may I offer you, both, my congratulations, but we must now think of propriety. Now that the princess is engaged, it is inappropriate for her to share any kind of confidence with a man other than her fiancé. The princess is most adept in picking up what's best for her. I feel sure you will come to understand each other very quickly.

LORD MARLBOROUGH   Suppose you're right. Must say you have been getting on my nerves. And now I speak the lingo a bit. *(to* **PRINCESS CARABOO***)* Zoolaki eh, Dolly?

Everyone laughs and toasts –

ALL   Zoolaki!

EDDIE   I think it is time I attended to some of my business interests abroad, I have been neglectful.

LORD MARLBOROUGH   *(barely listening)* As you wish, send us a pineapple for the wedding breakfast.

Only **PRINCESS CARABOO** *and* **LADY ELIZABETH** *notice* **EDDIE***'s distress.*

LADY ELIZABETH WORRALL   Edward – are you alright?

*   **LORD MARLBOROUGH** *and* **PRINCESS CARABOO** *are surrounded by well wishers who sing –*

GUESTS

> YOU'LL RULE THE WORLD, MY LORD.
> SHE'S SUCH A CATCH.
> ENGLISH ARISTOCRAT
> FINDS ROYAL MATCH,
> IT'S PERFECT.

> THE WEDDING WILL BE A SPECTACULAR
> – SPECIAL OCCASION
> EACH RELATION FULL OF PRIDE.

EDDIE

> WHY IS THIS HAPPENING?
> HOW IS THIS HAPPENING?
> WHERE AM I GOING TO HIDE?
> I CAN'T BEAR TO SEE,
> SOMEONE OTHER THEN ME –

CROWD *(to* **LORD MARLBOOUGH***)*
> NOW SHE'LL ALWAYS BE.

> **LORD MARLBOROUGH** *and* **PRINCESS CARABOO** *kiss.*
> YOUR BRIDE.

> **EDDIE** *is gone.*

> **OSVALDO AGATHIAS** *bursts in.*

OSVALDO AGATHIAS Your Lordship. Your Lordship. A word with you in private if I may.

LADY ELIZABETH WORRALL Charles! I do believe that's the rotter who stole our silver.

OSVALDO AGATHIAS I have some information you will want to hear. And if you don't I'm sure everyone else will.

SIR CHARLES WORRALL What is the meaning of this, sir?

OSVALDO AGATHIAS Shall we just say, I'm an old friend of the princess and I have some juicy gossip from the *(contemptuouly)* Royal House of Caraboo. All is not what it seems. Believe me, you'll want to hear what I have to say!

PRINCESS CARABOO *suddenly shrieks and begins pointing and incanting at* **OSVALDO AGATHIAS**.

PRINCESS CARABOO Ayahhgraiatalumis (etc!)

LORD MARLBOROUGH *(of* **OSVALDO AGATHIAS***)* Who is this oik? Get him out of here! He's upsetting my bride. *(To* **PRINCESS CARABOO***)* Steady there, Dolly. *(to* **OSVALDO AGATHIAS***)* Out with you I say! You're lucky I don't run you through. Show your face again around here and you won't be so fortunate.

The company hustle **OSVALDO AGATHIAS** *off stage. There is such commotion no one notices he sneaks back on through the crowd.*

OSVALDO AGATHIAS *(alone. With contempt)* Very well, your Lordship if you will not pay for my silence there are others who will pay me to sing like a canary. And you know what they say? When one little birdy starts to sing for his supper others soon follow.

SIR CHARLES WORRALL *in a spotlight.*

SIR CHARLES WORRALL Aracticus constructs for us a very elaborate mathematical equation equating the severity of being found out with the previous range and impact of the newly-exposed falsehood. Put simply: the bigger the stinker the greater the stench!

He exits.

Back to **OSVALDO AGATHIAS**.

OSVALDO AGATHIAS Oh, "My Lady", say goodbye to your fancy new life. From now, all thanks to me, there will be –

"SPITE"

DOWN IN A TAVERN ON FLEET STREET
I'LL HAVE 'EM BAYING FOR MORE!
TALES THAT I'M GOING TO SELL WILL
BRING MANY MORE TO THE FORE.
NEVER UNDERESTIMATE THE SPITEFULNESS OF
FOLK WHO WANT TO SETTLE A SCORE,
FLASH A LITTLE CASH AROUND
THE CHANCE OF SOME FAME
AND HEAR THE PUBLIC ROAR!

OSVALDO AGATHIAS *presents* **RICHARD** *as a* **REPORTER**.

OSVALDO AGATHIAS

VOILA!

REPORTER

I'M THE TIMES'S REPORTER

OSVALDO AGATHIAS

OLA! (*Trans. Hello*)

REPORTER

A SOURCE HAS CLAIMED.

OSVALDO AGATHIAS

PERDO? *(Trans. What?)*

REPORTER

THAT PRINCESS CARABOO'S A
TOTALLY FICTITIOUS NAME.

OSVALDO AGATHIAS

OH DIOS! *(Trans Oh God!)*

REPORTER

JUST A GIRL FROM DEVONSHIRE.

OSVALDO AGATHIAS

OLE!

REPORTER

WHO RAN AWAY.

GOSSIPS (HATTY, MRS CATESBY *and* **BETTY**) *enter.*

SPITEFUL CROOKS AND CHARLATANS LINE UP
TO BACK THE CLAIM!

GOSSIPS

SPITE COMING OUT OF THE WOODWORK,
SPITE COMING UP THROUGH THE FLOOR.

OSVALDO AGATHIAS

THE DEVIL'S THROWING A PARTY
FIENDS CONVENE AT EV'RY DOOR.

HATTY, MRS CATESBY and **BETTY**

NEVER UNDERESTIMATE THE SPITEFULNESS OF
FOLK WHO WANT TO SETTLE A SCORE.

REPORTER

FLASH A LITTLE CASH AROUND
THE CHANCE OF SOME FAME
AND HEAR THE PUBLIC ROAR!

GOSSIPS Well!

HATTY AS 1ST GOSSIP

SHE WAS A MAID BUT CRAVED
HER MASTER'S BED

OSVALDO AGATHIAS Diablo! (trans. Approximately - What
the devil?!)

MRS CATESBY AS 2ND GOSSIP

FLASHING HER ASSETS TILL
SHE TURNED HIS HEAD!

OSVALDO AGATHIAS Bravo!

BETTY AS 3RD GOSSIP

SHE HAD HIS BASTARD CHILD
ALL TWISTED, SO THEY SAID.

ALL THREE The little minx was like a jinx.

REPORTER Just as the Spaniard said.

ALL

SPITE

COMING OUT OF THE WOODWORK,
SPITE
COMING UP THROUGH THE FLOOR,
THE DEVIL'S THROWING A PARTY
FIENDS CONVENE AT EV'RY DOOR.
NEVER UNDERESTIMATE THE SPITEFULNESS OF
FOLK WHO WANT TO SETTLE A SCORE,
FLASH A LITTLE CASH AROUND
THE CHANCE OF SOME FAME
AND HEAR THE PUBLIC ROAR!

SIR CHARLES *steps in to narrate as* **LORD MARLBOROUGH** *reads* The Times *in horror as we hear* –

LORD MARLBOROUGH WHAT THE...?!

SIR CHARLES WORRALL AND IN THE HOMES OF THE GREAT.

LORD MARLBOROUGH HELL'S TEETH!

SIR CHARLES WORRALL THEY GET A FRIGHT.

LORD MARLBOROUGH *is replaced by* **LADY ELIZABETH WORRALL** *reading her paper.*

SIR CHARLES WORRALL THOSE WHO THE HARLOT HAS DUPED

NOW SEE THE LIGHT.

LADY ELIZABETH WORRALL CHARLES, COME QUICK

MY SMELLING SALTS.

SIR CHARLES WORRALL MY DEAR ARE YOU ALRIGHT?

Sight of the newspaper article stops him in mid-sentence.

OSVALDO AGATHIAS – TOUR THE LAND YOU WON'T BELIEVE

THE IMPACT

OF –

ALL

SPITE

COMING OUT OF THE WOODWORK,
SPITE –

Music continues.

LORD MARLOROUGH *confronts* **PRINCESS CARABOO**.

LORD MARLBOROUGH *(spoken)* Well, well. If it isn't my fairy
  princess. Doting on finery for our wedding my dear?
  (furious) I'll see you rot in hell first you –

He calls in time with the music.

  – Conniving, lying, manipulative bitch!

Whip! **(OSVALDO AGATHIAS** *hands it to him)*

*During the next verse he whips her to within an inch of
her life – a vicious and disturbing image probably best
suggested abstractly.*

Meanwhile **OSVALDO AGATHIAS** *crows in cruel delight
as all but* **LORD MARLBOROUGH** *and* **PRINCESS
CARABOO** *sing –*

ALL BUT LORD MARLBOROUGH AND PRINCESS CARABOO
  SHE'S A FIEND, SHE'S A FAKE, SHE'S A FRAUD
  SHE'S ROTTEN TO THE CORE!
  FLEECING THOSE WHO CARED FOR HER
  WHEREEVER SHE SAW FIT TO CALL.
  SHE DESERVES ALL SHE'S GOT COMING
  THERE'S NO MORE APPLAUSE –
  WE'LL FIX THAT CUNNING VIXEN NOW
  AND CLIP HER WICKED CLAWS.
  FOR SHE MUST LEARN SHE WILL GET BURNED
  IF SHE DARES TO IGNORE THE –

OSVALDO AGATHIAS Todo el mundo! *(trans: All together
  now!)*

ALL *(half time)*
  SPITE COMING OUT OF THE WOODWORK
  SPITE COMING UP THROUGH THE FLOOR

OSVALDO AGATHIAS

>   FANTASIST FANATICS

ALL

>   EVER'Y DAY BRINGS MORE AND MORE.
>   NEVER UNDERESTIMATE THE SPITEFULNESS OF
>   FOLK WHO WANT TO SETTLE A SCORE,
>   FLASH A LITTLE CASH AROUND
>   THE CHANCE OF SOME FAME
>   AND HEAR THE PUBLIC ROAR!
>
>   WHAT A CREATURE
>   WHAT A MESS
>   A CURSE, A PLAGUE, A BLIGHT!
>   IT SEEMS THE TALE OF PRINCESS CARABOO
>   WAS ALL A STEAMING CROCK OF –

LADY ELIZABETH WORRALL *(spoken)* It's not very nice, not very nice at all!

Musical resolve.

SPITE!

Effects. Thunder.

>   **PRINCESS CARABOO** *staggers out of* **LORD MARLBOROUGH***'s house into the rain.*
>
>   **A SERVANT**, **HATTY** *approaches her with a cloak.*

HATTY Miss, miss. You can't leave London, like this. I don't care what you've done. Take this cloak.

PRINCESS CARABOO *(shaking it off)* No. No. Thank you, Hatty. I arrived like a drowned rat in a thunderstorm, I'll leave that way too.

HATTY Where will you go?

PRINCESS CARABOO Back to the hall I s'pose. Where else is there for me?

Lights change to pick up **SIR CHARLES WORRALL**.

SIR CHARLES WORRALL Perhaps the most surprising lie classified by Aracticus in the library at Alexandria is what he terms the "non-lie". The lie one wishes one might tell, indeed should tell, the lie everyone expects to hear to maintain harmony. Yet this lie, for whatever reason, is never told, though the time has come for plain speaking.

Effects. We hear the sound of the bell at the **WORRALL** *residence.*

Lights up on **PRINCESS CARABOO** *standing at the door. The stormy night rages around her.*

BETTY *opens the door.*

BETTY *(not unsympathetic)* It's you, you come back...who'd have thought you'd come back here your Highn – your Maje – what'd I call you now?

PRINCESS CARABOO Mary, just Mary.

BETTY *(gawping)* Your clothes, they got blood on 'em. What they do to you? You're soaked. You never walked all the way from London? You'd better come in the dry.

SIR CHARLES WORRALL'S VOICE Betty? Who is it? It's past midnight. You know her Ladyship is ill.

He appears. Sees **PRINCESS CARABOO**. *Tenses up.*

That will be all, Betty.

Exit **BETTY**.

PRINCESS CARABOO Please, please forgive me... I'm so sorry.

SIR CHARLES WORRALL *(icily)* My dear, I'm afraid I must ask you to leave. Her Ladyship took the news of... of your...she took it very badly. She's not strong you see. Tragedy has made her vulnerable to those who… those who prey on the kind-hearted.

PRINCESS CARABOO I never meant for any of it. I didn't. I didn't. I swear.

SIR CHARLES WORRALL Well, my dear. We must at least admire your audacity in returning to this the scene of your crimes. But I should like you to go now. You have caused a lot of unhappiness here, a lot of heartbreak.

PRINCESS CARABOO I can't stand it! I never meant –

SIR CHARLES WORRALL My dear, if there is, if there is a shred of compassion in your heart for those you've hurt. I must ask you. No, no I must demand of you – never show your face here again. You will not be welcome. Goodbye. We shall not meet again.

He closes the door on her.

She falls to her knees.

PRINCESS CARABOO NO! *(she calls)* Your Ladyship! Sir Charles! *(biggest cry)* Eddie!

"WITHOUT YOUR LOVE"

(sings)

WITHOUT YOUR LOVE
HOW CAN I FACE THE MORNING AGAIN?
WITHOUT YOUR LOVE
HOW CAN I TOUCH THE SKY?
YOU PICKED ME UP AND PUT ME ON MY TWO FEET AGAIN
WITHOUT YOUR LOVE JUST WHO THE HELL AM I?

WITHOUT YOUR LOVE
I WALKED ALONE AFRAID OF THE DARK.
WITHOUT YOUR LOVE
THE WORLD WAS HARD TO BEAR.
WITHOUT YOUR LOVE I'M LIVING IN THE SHADOWS AGAIN
HOW CAN I GO ON WITH OUT YOU THERE?

WITHOUT YOUR LOVE
I'LL NEVER FEEL THE SUN ON MY FACE
WITHOUT YOUR LOVE
I DON'T KNOW WHO TO BE.
WITHOUT YOUR LOVE
WHERE WILL I KNOW THE PEACE THAT I FOUND
BELONGING HERE WITH YOU AS FAMILY.

I BEG YOU PLEASE
DON'T LET ME GO
I'M BEGGING NOW
PLEASE LET ME KNOW
WHAT I MUST DO FOR YOU TO FORGIVE ME BECAUSE
I'D DO ANYTHING FOR LIFE TO JUST GO BACK TO HOW IT
    WAS.

WITHOUT YOUR LOVE
HOW CAN I FACE THE MORNING AGAIN?
WITHOUT YOUR LOVE
HOW CAN I TOUCH THE SKY?
YOU PICKED ME UP AND PUT ME ON MY TWO FEET AGAIN
WITHOUT YOUR LOVE.

WITHOUT YOUR LOVE
WITHOUT YOUR LOVE
JUST WHO THE HELL AM I?

EDDIE *is there.*

EDDIE If you'll have me, you could be Mrs Mouse.

PRINCESS CARABOO Eddie! I thought you was… I thought you was gone abroad. I tried to get word to you but… they was watching me all the time. I didn't want to hurt you… Lord Marlborough, he didn't mean nothing to me –

EDDIE He meant a life of luxury to you even if you had to lie every day for the rest of your life.

PRINCESS CARABOO Don't judge me, everybody else judges me so harsh. Not you Eddie please.

EDDIE I can't afford to judge you. Not if I'm going to spend the rest of my life with you. And it seems like that's what I must do. Because I've tried to run far away and I just can't. I love you. And that means whatever you've done I have to try and forgive because if I don't... I... I want to be with you. Always.

PRINCESS CARABOO *(loving him)* You gurt wazzock.

EDDIE Marry me, but not out of pity, and not for what you can get out of me but...because... Do you think we can make each other happy?

PRINCESS CARABOO *(thinks, then –)* Yes, I reckon we could. But I've got to ask someone first.

EDDIE You've another admirer?

PRINCESS CARABOO No, its not that. I want... I need...well, I want to get someone's blessing.

Lights change and she turns.

EDDIE *is gone and she is facing* **LADY ELIZABETH WORRALL**, *looking tired, in her private sitting room.*

She holds up her hand.

LADY ELIZABETH WORRALL My dear, my dear. Stop talking. Draw breath for just a moment or your agitation will alert the servants. Sir Charles would not want you here. How on earth did you get in?

PRINCESS CARABOO Loads of what they say about me ain't true...but...well, it's true I know how to break into a place if I've a mind to.

LADY ELIZABETH WORRALL I see. What a complicated young woman you are. And now...now...you tell me you want my blessing to marry Edward. My advice, if you will. Edward is a very sensitive young man. It has always been my feeling that he needs protecting from the likes of...

PRINCESS CARABOO You should set the dogs on me.

LADY ELIZABETH WORRALL Yes, yes perhaps I should. But… I am…was a mother. You were too I understand. Oh, I've made some enquiries, records at the workhouse, talk of a daughter.

PRINCESS CARABOO *(quietly)* Alice.

LADY ELIZABETH WORRALL Alice. And she died, as my Charlotte died. So tell me… as mothers we need to ask ourselves –

"DAUGHTERS"

WHAT WOULD WE ADVISE OUR DAUGHTERS
IF THEY STOOD HERE BEFORE US NOW?
SO MANY THINGS WE MIGHT HAVE TAUGHT THEM
BUT THAT WAS SOMETHING HEAVEN COULDN'T, WOULDN'T
    ALLOW.
YET WHAT WOULD I ADVISE MY DAUGHTER
IF SHE STOOD HERE, AS YOU STAND HERE
ASKING ME TO HELP SOMEHOW?

KEEP HOLD OF THE TRUTH, THAT'S ALL YOU CAN DO
IF YOU LIVE A LIE, THAT WON'T EVER BE YOU.
WHEN YOU START TO PRETEND, YES YOU CAN GO FAR
BUT DO YOU REALLY WANT TO LIVE THAT LIFE,
REALLY WANT TO LIVE A LIE
LOSING SIGHT OF WHY YOU LIED
AND WHO YOU ARE?

PRINCESS CARABOO

SO YOU'D HAVE ME ADVISE MY DAUGHTER
TO KNOW HER PLACE, TO SCRAPE AND BOW
COWER IN THE COLD, CRUEL WORKHOUSE
IT'S EASY FOR YOU, WITH EVERYTHING MONEY ALLOWS.
IS THAT REALLY WHAT YOU'D TELL MY DAUGHTER?
IF SHE STOOD HERE, AS I STAND HERE
COULD YOU CRUSH HER DREAM OF HAPPINESS SOMEHOW?

LADY ELIZABETH WORRALL

KEEP HOLD OF THE TRUTH, THAT'S ALL WE CAN DO

YES I'VE BEEN SPOILT, I'M WEALTHY IT'S TRUE
BUT I ALSO HAD DREAMS AND YOU BROKE THEM IN TWO
WELL I SHOULD HAVE SEEN THE SCAM
BUT MY DEAR, I'M NOT A SHAM
I KNOW WHO I TRULY AM
DO YOU?

PRINCESS CARABOO

I AM MY OWN PERSON
NOBODY SPEAKS FOR ME
DON'T NEED ANOTHER STANDING IN MY STEAD NOW
I HAVE MY OWN FEELINGS
AND MY DREAMS BELONG TO ME
DON'T NEED NO-ONE TO SAY "YOU GO AHEAD NOW".

AND TO EVERYONE WHO'D HOLD ME BACK
AND TELL ME TAKE IT SLOW
WELL LET ME TELL YOU THEY DON'T REALLY KNOW ME.
I'VE HAD ENOUGH OF HOLDING BACK
NOT TREADING ON THEIR TOES
I DON'T NEED YOU OR ANYONE TO SHOW ME
WHO I COULD BE.

Music doesn't resolve.

LADY ELIZABETH WORRALL My dear, do you have your
answer? Do you know what you should do?

Cut to **EDDIE** *and* **SIR CHARLES WORRALL** *in a rather
bleak chapel.*

EDDIE So, the exotic Princess Caraboo is to become my wife
in this drafty chapel. Have you come to disapprove, Sir
Charles? You need not. I know your feelings.

SIR CHARLES WORRALL Edward, my boy. This is a cheerless
place. If you are determined to go through with this
marriage I owe it to your mother's memory to at least
try and make it a pleasant occasion with a few candles
from the Hall. *(To servants off)* Servants, if you please.

HATTY, BETTY, MRS CATESBY *and* **RICHARD** *and*
OTHER SERVANTS *enter.*

ALL BUT EDDIE

> THE WEDDING WE THOUGHT WE WOULD NEVER SEE
> A LITTLE CHAPEL IN THE SNOW
> HOW'S HE FORGIVEN HER?
> YET HE'S FORGIVEN HER
> SO SHOULDN'T WE FORGIVE HER SO?

BETTY

> THE WEDDING OF THE PRINCESS CARABOO
> A LOVE BY ANY OTHER NAME
> IF EDDIE SEES THE GOOD,
> THOUGH NO-ONE'S UNDERSTOOD,
> WELL THEN WE ALL SHOULD DO THE SAME.

ALL

> AND JESU CHRIST CAME DOWN TO EARTH FOR US
> TO WASH OUR MANY SINS AWAY
> SO EV'RY MAN AND WIFE
> BEGIN A MARRIED LIFE
> UPON THEIR WEDDING DAY.
> HE HAS FORGIVEN ALL
> HER TRESPASSES
> IN HARMONY THE TWO ARE TIED
> A SACRED CHERISHING
> NEEDS NO EMBELLISHING
> FOREVER SIDE BY SIDE.

And the place is beautiful with little candles.

EDDIE Thank you all, it's perfect. So beautiful for my beautiful bride. Where can she be?

Clock strikes the quarter.

(uneasy) Late… Well, a bride's prerogative.

The chapel door creaks open.

And here she is.

*Everyone turns to the door but it's **LADY ELIZABETH WORRALL**.*

LADY ELIZABETH WORRALL No, Edward. It's me.

EDDIE You came, I didn't think you would. Do you think you can come to forgive her?

LADY ELIZABETH WORRALL I have… I have some rather startling news for you.

They stare at each other.

Lights down on them. Up on **LORD MARLBOROUGH** *with his* **MANSERVANT**.

LORD MARLBOROUGH I want the Cheltenham house prepared for our arrival. The blue room is to be redecorated for my wife. With orchids.

MANSERVANT Your wife, sir?

LORD MARLBOROUGH Yes, boy, that's what I said. By this time tomorrow there will be a Lady Marlborough as planned.

MANSERVANT But we were told the wedding was… Her Highness…was not to be admitted.

LORD MARLBOROUGH The Former Princess Caraboo and I have come to an understanding. I found I… I found I… (missed her). Without her I… Something missing, a light went out…a… I sought her out.*(Toughening up again)* Mind your own business, damn you!

MANSERVANT I'm sorry, sir. I… Congratulations, your Lordship.

LORD MARLBOROUGH Get on with your work or I'll have you gelded.

MANSERVANT *exits.*

Lights back to the chapel.

LADY ELIZABETH WORRALL *hands* **EDDIE** *a note.*

EDDIE What's this?

He takes the note and looks at it unopened.

Is it from her?

LADY ELIZABETH WORRALL *nods.*

Lights down on them.

Lights up on **OSVALDO AGATHIAS** *with* **MEG,** *the chattering London inn servant.*

MEG What's the matter?

OSVALDO AGATHIAS Look at the state of this room. It's disgusting. Tonight I marry a gracious lady. You think she wants to spend a wedding night in this pig sty? And air the mattress, let the lice get a little sunlight. My wife-to-be, she is used to…she…she was once a princess.

MEG See what you mean. This'll be a bit of a come-down.

OSVALDO AGATHIAS But she loves me, you understand, she still loves me. After everything. That's why I pick her up out of the gutter. I use my last money, my last everything to buy us a passage out of this stinking country. I will not trouble you with my presence for very much longer.

Back to the chapel.

SIR CHARLES WORRALL Elizabeth, what does it say? Is it from that wretched girl?

EDDIE *is still staring at the unopened letter.*

Edward?

Back to **LORD MARLBOROUGH** *and* **MANSERVANT**.

MANSERVANT Sir, there's a letter for you. Delivered to the back door.

LORD MARLBOROUGH *snatches it and tears it open to read.*

LORD MARLBOROUGH *(furious)* She's tricked me! Damn her! Bitch! *(to the servant)* Check the safe. Tell me how much money is missing.

Exits.

Back in **OSVALDO AGATHIAS***'s room.*

OSVALDO AGATHIAS *(a letter in his hand)* What's this letter? It's addressed to me. Why no-one give this to me before?

He begins to read it.

(to **MEG***. Off)* The woman, the woman, who left this. What way did she go? How long ago was she here? *(As he exits)* I need to get to the ship. That witch has stolen our tickets. I need to get to the dock before it's too late.

Back to the chapel.

EDDIE *still hasn't opened the letter.*

EDDIE *(to* **LADY ELIZABETH WORRALL***)* She's not coming is she?

LADY ELIZABETH WORRALL I'm afraid not, my dear.

EDDIE I should have known, the moment she said "yes" that she'd never turn up.

EDDIE, THE WORRALLS, LORD MARLBOROUGH *and* **OSVALDO AGATHIAS** *sing gently in harmony.*

"CONCLUSION"

SHE WAS HER OWN PERSON
NOBODY SPOKE FOR HER
NEVER NEEDED ANYONE TO GUIDE HER

SHE HAD HER OWN FEELINGS
AND HER DREAMS BELONGED TO HER
SHE HID HER REAL FEELINGS DEEP INSIDE HER.

LORD MARLBOROUGH *and* **OSVALDO AGATHIAS** *exit.*

Music continues from now until the end.

LADY ELIZABETH WORRALL   Edward, please. Won't you
open the letter?

Finally he does.

Momentum underscore.

After a while.

SIR CHARLES WORRALL What is it Edward?

But **EDDIE** *rushes out followed by the others.*

Lights up on the deck of the ship.

*Momentum music gives way to the soothing sound of a
ship at sea.*

PRINCESS CARABOO *staring at the horizon much as she
looked when we first saw her.*

SAILOR'S VOICE FROM OFF   America, America to starboard!

PRINCESS CARABOO *sings to herself –*
AND TO EVERYONE WHO'D HOLD ME BACK
AND TELL ME TAKE IT SLOW.
WELL LET ME TELL YOU THEY DON'T REALLY KNOW ME.
I'VE HAD ENOUGH OF HOLDING BACK
NOT TREADING ON THEIR TOES
I DON'T NEED THEM OR ANYONE TO SHOW ME
WHO I SHOULD BE.

Music swells.

EDDIE *enters similarly bundled against the cold.*

EDDIE Are you warm enough, Mrs Mouse?

PRINCESS CARABOO I am, Mr Mouse.

EDDIE A new life in America. No more pretending.

PRINCESS CARABOO A fresh start.

EDDIE No more lies. Mary, you know I can't afford…there will be no orchids on this adventure. Just hard work and hope.

PRINCESS CARABOO This ship's full of hope. All people who've turned their back on the past. All ready to make a new start, people like us that won't be beaten down.

EDDIE I love you.

PRINCESS CARABOO I love you. Thank you for not listening to those others. That was quite a fuss they was all making at the gangplank.

EDDIE Now, why would I listen to them?

PRINCESS CARABOO Her Ladyship understood.

EDDIE Yes, I believe she did.

PRINCESS CARABOO Eddie, I'm ready for our big adventure.

They stand in each other's arms and look at the horizon and sing triumphantly.

BOTH
I AM MY OWN PERSON
I NEED NOBODY BUT YOU
WE CAN FACE WHATEVER FATE DECIDES NOW.
THOUGH THINGS WON'T BE EASY
AT LAST I'M STRONG ENOUGH
STANDING PROUD WITH YOU HERE AT MY SIDE NOW.

PRINCESS CARABOO

> I WAS ALWAYS TROUBLE
> NOW I'M GONNA DO MY BEST
> TO SETTLE DOWN AND TRY TO BE A GOOD WIFE.

EDDIE

> YOU TAUGHT ME A MAN
> SHOULD ALWAYS FIGHT FOR WHAT HE WANTS,
> SO I VOW I'LL BUILD US BOTH A GOOD LIFE.

SAILOR'S VOICE FROM OFF Immigration boarding, have your papers ready!

PASSENGER We made it! We made it to America!

The stage fills with the whole company as immigrants arriving in America. all singing triumphantly –

ALL

> TAKE A CHANCE
> LEAD THE DANCE
> COME ON AND JOIN ME
> FEEL THE BEAT
> STAND TALL AND PROUD AND SAY –
>
> I AM MY OWN PERSON
> NOBODY SPEAKS FOR ME
> DON'T NEED ANOTHER STANDING IN MY STEAD NOW
> I HAVE MY OWN FEELINGS
> AND MY DREAMS BELONG TO ME
> DON'T NEED NO ONE TO SAY YOU GO AHEAD NOW.
>
> CAN'T YOU LEAVE THE PAST BEHIND
> AND FOLLOW –

EDDIE *(to* **PRINCESS CARABOO***)* Wait here, I'll get Sir Charles's letter of recommendation for the authorities.

EDDIE *exits*

SIR CHARLES WORRALL *appears in a spotlight.*

SIR CHARLES WORRALL And so we reach the end of our little meditation on lying and liars inspired by the musing of the great and worthy Aracticus all those centuries ago. Are we any wiser do you suppose? Better equipped to protect ourselves from deception or spot a fake? I think not. Much of this tale is based on actual events, more then you might imagine, but can you tease the truth from a fiction spun together for your entertainment? And why would you? For some lies are pleasant to believe in. For instance the philosopher Aracticus. There was no such man. I made the whole thing up. Yet you nodded sagely when I mentioned him because it pleased you to think yourself cleverer then you are. It quite saddens me to disillusion you.

Lights down on him.

Back on the deck of the ship an **AMERICAN IMMIGRATION OFFICER** *appears and speaks to* **CARABOO**.

AMERICAN IMMIGRATION OFFICER Immigration. Welcome to America. May I check you papers ma'am?

She stares at him.

Your papers, do you speak English miss?

No response.

I need to see your papers. What's your name? You've got a name ain't yah?

EDDIE *returns just in time to see her point to herself and say –*

PRINCESS CARABOO   *(as if in broken English)* Caraboo, Princess Caraboo.

Blackout on **EDDIE**'*s despair.*

Music resolves.

The End

Property List

Blunderbuss (p11)

Knife (p12)

Silverware (p12)

Gun (p12)

Atlas (p21)

Engravings (p26)

Champagne (p36)

Easel (p49)

The Times newspaper (p71)

Whip (p72)

Note (p81)

Letter (p82)

Letter (p83)

Costume:

Sir Charles Worrall – Home-made Maharajah outfit (p23)

Women – Arabic fancy dress (p25)

Hatty – carrying cloak (p73)

Lighting

Spotlight (p1)

Lights restore to normal (p13)

Spotlight (p16)

Lights change to gloom (p19)

Lights up (p20)

Lights change (p25)

Sudden spotlight on Sir Charles Worrall (p27)

Back to normality (p27)

Lights change (p29)

Spotlight (p32)

Lights change (p32)

Lights change (p34)

Spotlight (p40)

Spotlight (p47)

Spotlight (p54)

Sound and lights take us to London (p55)

Spotlight (p57)

Spotlight (p67)

Lights change (p74)

Lights up on Princess Caraboo (p74)

Lights change (p77)

Candlelight (p80)

Lights down (p81)

Lights back to the chapel (p81)

Lights down on them (p82)

Lights up on the deck of the ship (p84)

Spotlight (p86)

Lights down on him (p87)

Blackout (p87)

Sound/Effects

Thunder and lighting (p6)

Shot (p11)

Shot (p12)

Sound and lights take us to London (p55)

Thunder (p73)

Bell (p74)

Clock strikes the quarter (p80)

Soothing sound of a ship at sea (p84)

Lightning Source UK Ltd.
Milton Keynes UK
UKOW06f0038010416

271297UK00001B/5/P